Microsoft® Access 2016

by Brian Favro

LEVEL 1

LABYRINTH LEARNING™

Microsoft Access 2016: Level 1

Labyrinth Learning
2560 9th Street, Suite 320
Berkeley, California 94710
800.522.9746
On the web at lablearning.com

Product Manager:
Jason Favro

Development Manager:
Laura Popelka

Senior Editor:
Alexandra Mummery

Junior Editor:
Alexandria Henderson

Assessment and Multimedia Content Development:
Ben Linford, Judy Mardar, Andrew Vaughnley

Production Manager:
Debra Grose

Compositor:
Happenstance Type-O-Rama

Indexer:
Valerie Perry

Interior Design:
Debra Grose

Cover Design:
Mick Koller

ebook only ITEM: 1-59136-869-3
ISBN-13: 978-159136-869-4

ebook with printed textbook ITEM: 1-59136-870-7
ISBN-13: 978-159136-870-0

Manufactured in the United States of America

GPP 10 9 8 7 6 5 4 3

Table of Contents

Preface iv

Access 2016 Chapter 1: Getting Started with Tables

Introducing Databases 2
Types of Databases 2
Open and Save an Access Database 3
Database Objects and the Access Window 3
Introducing Tables 6
Table Features 6
Field Data Types 7
Primary Key Fields 7
Creating a Table in a New Database 7
Creating Tables in Design View 9
Field Properties 9
Sorting and Filtering Table Data 11
Importing Data Sources 12
Relational Databases 13
Referential Integrity 13
Data Normalization 13
Reinforce Your Skills 15
Apply Your Skills 18
Extend Your Skills 20

Access 2016 Chapter 2: Working with Forms

Creating Forms 22
Record Sources 22
Creating and Using Basic Forms 23
Creating Forms with the Form Wizard 23
Changing Forms in Layout View 24
Changing Forms in Design View 26
Modify the Form Header Section 26
Tab Order 28
Themes 29
Creating Other Types of Forms 30
Creating Multiple Item Forms 30
Creating Split Forms 31
Reinforce Your Skills 32
Apply Your Skills 35
Extend Your Skills 38

Access 2016 Chapter 3: Querying a Database

Select Queries 40
Query Features 40
Creating a Select Query Using Query Design View 42
Designing a Query Using Multiple Tables 43
Choosing Fields to Include in a Query 43
Selecting a Field That Appears in Multiple Tables 43
Using Criteria in Queries 44
Wildcard Characters 46
AND and OR Criteria 46
Date Criteria 47
Sorting, Showing, and Limiting Results 49
Limiting the Number of Results Displayed 49
Calculated Fields 50
Identifying Parts of a Calculated Field 50
Calculated Field Properties 51
Reinforce Your Skills 53
Apply Your Skills 58
Extend Your Skills 62

Access 2016 Chapter 4: Using Reports to Display Information

Introducing Reports 64
Basic Reports 64
Report Organization and Structure 65
Sections 65
Grouping and Sorting 66
The Report Wizard 66
Modifying Reports 68
Controls 68
Adding Fields to a Report 68
Header and Footer Objects 72
Formatting Controls 74
Themes 77
Reinforce Your Skills 78
Apply Your Skills 85
Extend Your Skills 89

Glossary 91
Index 93

Preface

This textbook is part of our brand-new approach to learning for introductory computer courses. We've kept the best elements of our proven instructional design and added powerful, interactive elements and assessments that offer enormous potential to engage learners in a new way. We're delighted with the results, and we hope that learners and educators are, too!

Why Did We Write This Content?

In today's digital world, knowing how to use the most common software applications is critical, and those who don't are left behind. Our goal is to simplify the entire learning experience and help every student develop the practical, real-world skills needed to be successful at work and in school. Using a combination of text, videos, interactive elements, and assessments, we begin with fundamental concepts and take learners through a systematic progression of exercises to reach mastery.

What Key Themes Did We Follow?

We had conversations with dozens of educators at community colleges, vocational schools, and other learning environments in preparation for this textbook. We listened and have adapted our learning solution to match the needs of a rapidly changing world, keeping the following common themes in mind:

Keep it about skills. Our content focus is on critical, job-ready topics and tasks, with a relentless focus on practical, real-world skills and common sense as well as step-by-step instruction to ensure that learners stay engaged from the first chapter forward. We've retained our proven method of progressively moving learners through increasingly independent exercises to ensure mastery—an approach that has been successfully developing skills for more than 20 years.

Keep it simple. Our integrated solutions create a seamless and engaging experience built on a uniquely dynamic instructional design that brings clarity to even the most challenging topics. We've focused our content on the things that matter most and have presented it in the easiest way for today's learners to absorb it. Concise chunks of text are combined with visually engaging and interactive elements to increase understanding for all types of learners.

Keep it relevant. Fresh, original, and constantly evolving content helps educators keep pace with today's student and work environments. We have reviewed every topic for relevancy and have updated it where needed to offer realistic examples and projects for learners.

How Do I Use This Book?

We understand that we are in a time of transition and that some students will still appreciate a print textbook to support their learning. Our comprehensive learning solution consists of a groundbreaking interactive ebook for primary content delivery and our easy-to-use eLab course management tool for assessment. We want to help students as they transition to a digital solution. Our interactive ebook contains learning content delivered in ways that will engage learners. Students can utilize a print text supplement in conjunction with the ebook that provides all the textual elements from the ebook in a full-color, spiral-bound print format.

Our eLab platform provides additional learning content such as overviews for each chapter, automatically graded projects and other assessments that accurately assess student skills, and clear feedback and analytics on student actions.

Included with Your Textbook Purchase

- *Interactive ebook*: A dynamic, engaging, and truly interactive textbook that includes elements such as videos, self-assessments, slide shows, and other interactive features. Highlighting, taking notes, and searching for content is easy.
- *eLab Course Management System*: A robust tool for accurate assessment, tracking of learner activity, and automated grading that includes a comprehensive set of instructor resources. eLab can be fully integrated with your LMS, making course management even easier.
- *Instructor resources*: This course is also supported on the Labyrinth website with a comprehensive instructor support package that includes detailed lesson plans, PowerPoint presentations, a course syllabus, test banks, additional exercises, and more.
- *Learning Resource Center*: The exercise files that accompany this textbook can be found within eLab and on the Learning Resource Center, which may be accessed from the ebook or online at **www.labyrinthelab.com/lrc**.
- *Overview chapter content*: The "Overview Chapter ISM" folder in the Instructor Support Materials package and the "Overview Chapter Files" folder in the Student Exercise File download include the helpful "Introducing Microsoft Office and Using Common Features" chapter. In addition to providing a discussion of the various Office versions, this chapter introduces a selection of features common throughout the Office applications. **We recommend that students complete this "overview" chapter first.**

We're excited to share this innovative, new approach with you, and we'd love you to share your experience with us at www.lablearning.com/share.

Display Settings

Multiple factors, including screen resolution, monitor size, and window size, can affect the appearance of the Microsoft Ribbon and its buttons. In this textbook, screen captures were taken at the native (recommended) screen resolutions in Office 2016 running Windows 10, with ClearType enabled.

Visual Conventions

This book uses visual and typographic cues to guide students through the lessons. Some of these cues are described below.

Cue Name	What It Does
`Type this text`	Text you type at the keyboard is printed in this typeface.
Action words	The important action words in exercise steps are presented in boldface.
Ribbon	Glossary terms are highlighted with a light yellow background.
Note! Tip! Warning!	Tips, notes, and warnings are called out with special icons.
!	Videos and WebSims that are a required part of this course are indicated by this icon.
Command→Command→ Command→Command	Commands to execute from the Ribbon are presented like this: Ribbon Tab→Command Group→Command→Subcommand.
Design→Themes→Themes	These notes present shortcut steps for executing certain tasks.

Acknowledgements

Many individuals contribute to the development and completion of a textbook. This book has benefited significantly from the feedback and suggestions of the following reviewers:

Pam Silvers, *Asheville-Buncombe Technical Community College*

Ramiro Villareal, *Brookhaven College*

Teresa Loftis, *Inland Career Education Center*

Kim Pigeon, *Northeast Wisconsin Technical College*

Lynne Kemp, *North Country Community College*

Tom Martin, *Shasta College*

Karen LaPlant, *Hennepin Technical College*

Kay Gerken, *College of DuPage*

Colleen Kennedy, *Spokane Community College*

ACCESS

1 Getting Started with Tables

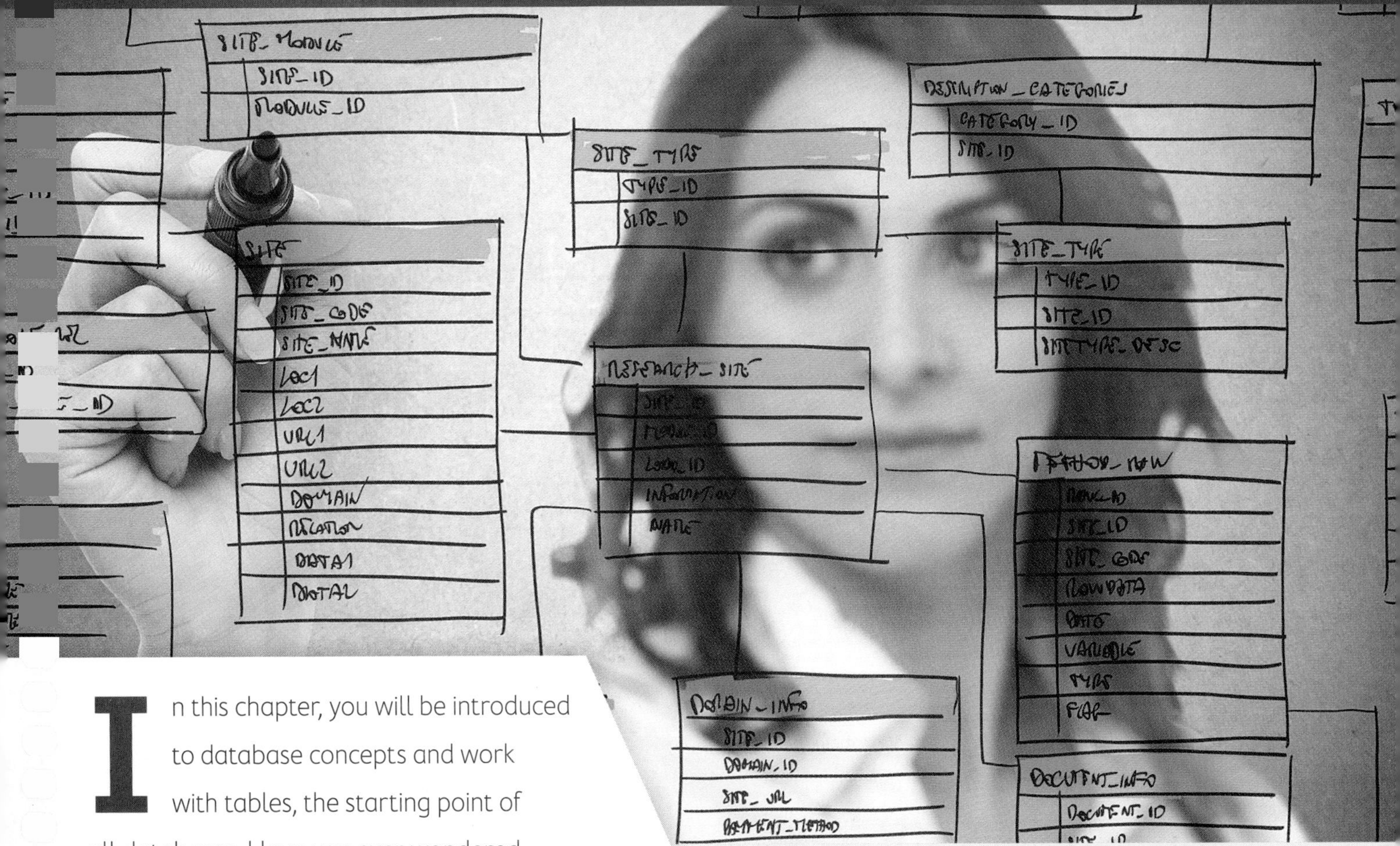

In this chapter, you will be introduced to database concepts and work with tables, the starting point of all databases. Have you ever wondered how sportscasters come up with fun and interesting facts about teams and players in a flash? Have you been taken by surprise when a customer service agent suddenly begins to recite your name, address, and a detailed purchase history? In most cases, these people have access to a powerful database from which they obtain the information.

LEARNING OBJECTIVES

- Identify database objects and the functions they perform
- Identify table features
- Create database tables
- Identify and choose data types
- Sort and filter table records
- Import a data source
- Establish a relationship between two database tables

Project: Creating a Database

Winchester Web Design is a small website development company. The company specializes in building websites for small businesses. You have been asked to build a database to help the company manage its employee, customer, and sales data. You'll get started by creating a database and building tables and table relationships.

Introducing Databases

It is likely that you routinely interact with databases. If you make an online purchase, your order information goes into a database. The database might be used to track your order status, product likes and reviews, past orders, or future promotions. If you post or like something on your Facebook account, that information is maintained in a database. If you search for or store a telephone number, that information is likely kept in a database. It is quite possible you have been using databases without even knowing it! Here, you will be introduced to what a database is and gain a better understanding of related terms, explore a sample database, and finally, create your own!

While there are many definitions of a database, you can think of a database as an organized collection of related data files or tables. For example, a company might organize its information by both customers (external to the business) and employees (internal to the business). While the data relate to the same business, the types of data provided for customers and employees will likely differ.

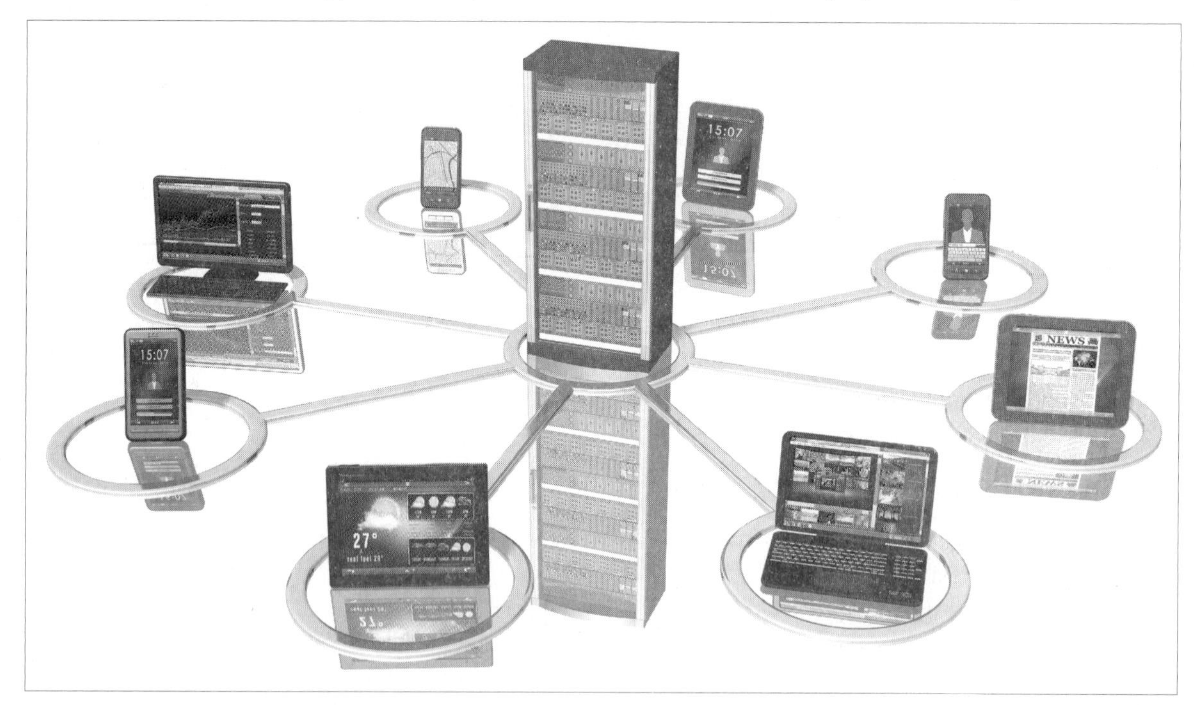

Databases are the epicenter of our digital world.

Types of Databases

Large organizations typically use large custom-designed databases specifically for that company or industry. When you make travel plans, you are using a database that is specific to the airline industry. It contains real-time data, meaning that if there is only one seat left on a plane, whoever selects and pays for the seat first gets the reservation. If you are a small business owner, you may use a database like Microsoft Access to track information about your customers, products, and employees. Access provides the tools needed to let small organizations create, use, and maintain databases.

Open and Save an Access Database

Each time you start Access, the Backstage view displays options for opening an existing file, creating a new blank database, or selecting from a number of pre-built templates. If you're creating a new database, Access will immediately prompt you to save the file in your desired storage location. You must save your file first because the database needs to constantly make updates to data as it is entered or edited.

DEVELOP YOUR SKILLS: A1-D1

In this exercise, you will open an existing Access database and save it with a new name.

Before You Begin: *Be sure to visit the Learning Resource Center at labyrinthelab.com/lrc to retrieve the exercise files for this course before beginning this exercise.*

1. Click **Start**.
2. Type `Ac` and then choose **Access 2016** from the list of suggestions.
3. Browse through the list of templates and then choose **Open Other Files** near the lower-left side of the window.
4. Click the **Browse** button, navigate to your **Access Chapter 1** folder, and double-click the **A1-D1-WinWebDesign** database file.
5. Click **Enable Content** if the Security Warning bar displays.

   The Security Warning appears whenever a database file is opened for the first time. You should never open files unless you know and trust the file sender. The database objects are shown in the Navigation pane on the left.
6. Choose **File→Save As**.
7. Click **Save As** to accept Access Database as the file type.
8. Add `Revised` to the end of the filename making it `A1-D1-WinWebDesignRevised` and click the **Save** button.

   The database is saved as a Microsoft Access Database file type. This format saves databases as Access 2007–2016 files with the file extension of .accdb.
9. Click **Enable Content** when the Security Warning bar displays again.

   Not only did you save the database with a new name, which creates another file, but you also closed the original database and opened the new one so the Security Warning appears again.
10. Keep Access open, as you will continue to use the database to explore the Access environment.

Note! *Always leave the database file open at the end of an exercise unless instructed to close it.*

Database Objects and the Access Window

The Access window includes the Ribbon, Navigation pane, and work area. A database object is a structure used to either store or retrieve data. The four Access objects are tables, queries, forms, and reports. The database objects are displayed in the Navigation pane on the left side of the window. The work area is where you create or modify database objects.

DATABASE OBJECT TYPES	
Access Object	**What It Does**
Table	Tables contain the database's data, and they let you enter, edit, delete, or view records in a row and column layout that is similar to that used in an Excel worksheet.
Form	Forms are used to view, edit, and add data one table record at a time.
Query	Queries are used to search for specific table records using criteria and to sort and perform calculations on the results.
Report	Reports are printable database objects that can display, group, and summarize data from tables and/or queries.

View the video "Working with Access Objects."

DEVELOP YOUR SKILLS: A1-D2

In this exercise, you will open and view the four Access object types.

1. Take a moment to explore the Access window noticing the various tables, queries, forms, and reports in the Navigation pane.

Explore a Table

2. Double-click the **Customers** table in the Objects list of the Navigation pane to open it in the work area within Datasheet View.

   Notice that the table, which is in Datasheet View, looks like a worksheet with columns and rows. Datasheet View lets you view, add, and edit table records. One benefit of Datasheet View is it lets you see more than one record at a time.

3. Click in the **first empty Cust ID** cell at the bottom of the CustID column.
4. Type **AdamsA** and tap Tab to complete the entry and move the insertion point to the next field.

   Notice the pencil icon highlighted in yellow. This indicates the current record is active and being created or edited.

	⊞ ThibeauxP	Thibeaux	Pierre
	⊞ WinklerS	Winkler	Samuel
✎	⊞ AdamsA		
*			

   Cust ID is known as a primary key field in this table, so each Cust ID must be unique.

5. Type **Adams** in the Last Name field and tap Tab.
6. Enter **Anthony** as the First Name, **23 Pine St** as the street address, and **Bradenton** as the city.
7. Click the **drop-down menu** button ▼ in the ST field and choose **FL** from the list of states.

   ST is an example of a field with properties that make data entry easy and accurate.

8. Complete the record as follows, making sure you tap Tab after entering the information.

   Tapping Tab after entering data completes the record, saving it in the database. As you enter the telephone number, Access will automatically format the entry for you.

- ZIP: **34210**
- Telephone: **(941) 555-3648**
- Email: **AAdams@email.com**
- Notes: **Call for delivery.**

9. Choose **Home→Views→View menu button ▼** and then choose **Design View**.

   Each object type can be created or edited using Design View. Tables Design View is where fields can be added, removed, or edited and field properties can be set.

10. Click the **View menu** button ▼ and choose **Datasheet View**.

    Notice the Anthony Adams record is now the second record in the table. It moved up because the records are sorted in ascending order using the Cust ID field.

Explore a Form

Now you will explore a form that is based on the Customers table. Forms help facilitate effective data entry by displaying one record at a time.

11. Double-click **Customers Form** in the Forms section of the Navigation pane.

    Notice the form displays all fields from the Customers table but only one record is visible.

12. Locate the Record bar at the bottom of the form.

    Record: |◀ ◀ 1 of 16 ▶ ▶| ▶*

13. Click the **Next Record** ▶ button to view the Anthony Adams record you just entered.
14. Click in the **Notes** box and add the phrase **after 10:00** to the end of the note (that is, "Call for Delivery after 10:00").
15. Click the **Next Record** ▶ button again to complete the edit.

    This edit has now been saved in the Customers table.

Explore a Query

Now you will explore a query that is based on the Customers table. Queries choose specific database records using criteria that you specify.

16. Double-click **Customers Query** in the Queries section of the Navigation pane.

    The query results look like a table displayed in Datasheet View, but the query only displays some of the fields from the underlying Customers table and records where the City is equal to Bradenton.

17. Click the **View menu** button ▼ on the Ribbon and choose **Design View**.

    The query has fields from the Customers table and the criterion bradenton. *This is an example of a simple query based on a single table. Queries can draw data from multiple tables and can include more sophisticated criteria.*

18. Choose **Design→Results→Run** ! to run the query and display only the Bradenton results.

Explore a Report

Now you will explore a report that uses multiple tables, including the Customers table.

19. Double-click **Invoice Details Report** in the Reports section.

    Take a moment to scroll through and observe the report.

20. Switch to **Design View** .

    The Report design grid may look complicated, but it's easy to create a robust report using the Access Report Wizard. The design grid can then be used to make modifications once the foundation has been set with the Wizard.

21. Switch to **Report View** , which is great for viewing reports.
22. Follow these steps to explore the object tabs and to close an object:

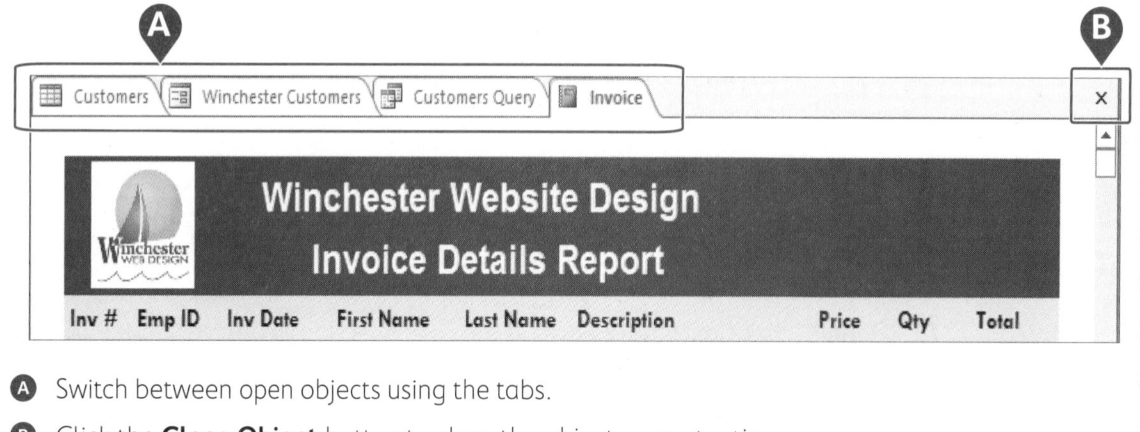

    Ⓐ Switch between open objects using the tabs.

    Ⓑ Click the **Close Object** button to close the objects one at a time.

23. Choose **File→Close** to close the database.

Introducing Tables

A table is the starting point for entering, finding, and reporting useful information located in your database. A database can have separate tables, each tracking different types of data. A business might use a table to keep track of customer billing or employee contact information.

Table Features

Data are meaningful units of information such as names, numbers, dates, and descriptions organized for reference or analysis. The data stored in the Winchester Web Design Group database might include customer first and last names, business names, telephone numbers, and other important information.

A field is the smallest meaningful unit of information about one person, place, or item. Individually, each field represents a piece of data. Together the fields provide information. In most databases fields are displayed in columns.

A record is a collection of related fields about a person, place, or item, such as a single customer or employee. A collection of related records makes up a table. In most databases records are displayed in rows.

Customers Table

Cust ID	Last Name	First Name	Street Address	City	ST	ZIP	Telephone
AndersM	Anders	Mark	205 Montana St	Bradenton	FL	34205	(941) 555-2309
DavisP	Davis	Peter	65 Terracotta Wa	Sarasota	FL	34228	(941) 555-1792
JeffriesD	Jeffries	Daniel	102 South Fern St	Bradenton	FL	34209	(941) 555-6939
RobertsJ	Roberts	John	103 Pine Terrace	Sarasota	FL	34232	(941) 555-7820
SantosE	Santos	Emily	33 Fairview Lane	Bradenton	FL	34210	(941) 555-1029
SmithW	Smith	William	879 Fifteenth Ave	Bradenton	FL	34210	(941) 555-0793

First Name field and JeffriesD record in Customers table

Field Data Types

If you have ever filled out an online form, you might have seen instant formatting of some fields. When typing in currency values, the dollar sign and decimal point may appear automatically, and when entering a date, the slashes between month, day, and year spontaneously appear. This can be accomplished by assigning a data type to the field. A data type sets the characteristics of a particular field, identifying the type of values it may hold, such as alphanumeric text, or numbers, or dates, yes/no values, or even a hyperlink.

Primary Key Fields

Almost every database table should have a primary key field. A primary key is a unique identifier for each record in the table. Examples of fields that would make good primary keys are Social Security numbers, student IDs, or email addresses. Using a student ID as a primary key ensures that each student is uniquely identified in a student database table. Two students may have identical names, but they will never have identical student ID numbers.

Design→Tools→Primary Key

Creating a Table in a New Database

Instead of using a database that someone else has prepared, you can design your own using a blank database template in Access. Tables are the starting point for databases and this shows up when a new blank database is first created. The new table has a single primary key field as a starting point for the database.

Table1

	ID	Click to Add
*	(New)	

The starting point in a blank database

ACCESS

DEVELOP YOUR SKILLS: A1-D3

In this exercise, you will create a new blank database and add an Invoices table in Datasheet View.

1. Choose **File→New→Blank Desktop Database**.
2. Click **Browse Folders** and save the database in your **Access Chapter 1 folder** as `A1-D3-Datasheet`.

3. Click the **Create** button, and a new table will appear.
4. Follow these steps to change the name of the ID field and set the data type for a second field:

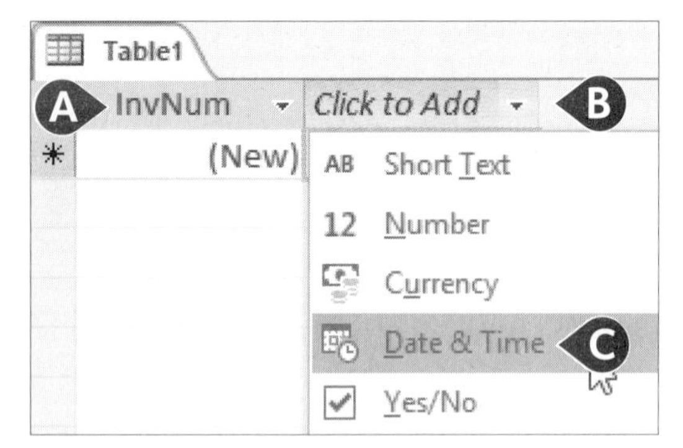

Ⓐ Double-click the **ID** field name and type **`InvNum`** as the new name. This will be the primary key field.

Ⓑ Tap [Tab] to go to the second column and, if necessary, choose **Click to Add** to display the data type list.

Ⓒ Choose **Date & Time**.

Once the data type is selected, the heading for the new field becomes Field1.

5. Replace *Field1* with the name **`InvDate`** and tap [Tab] to move to a new field.

   Your table currently has a primary key field and one Date/Time field.

6. Choose **Short Text** as the data type for the third field and change the field name to **`EmpID`**.
7. Tap [Tab], choose **Short Text** for the fourth field data type, and change the field name to **`CustID`**.

   Your simple table with four fields is now set up and ready for data to be entered.

8. Click in the **empty InvDate** field (you might have to click twice) and type **`12/15/2016`**.
9. Tap [Tab] and type **`JFW`** as the EmpID.
10. Tap [Tab] and type **`SmithW`** as the CustID.
11. Enter the data for these three additional records:

    The InvNum primary key field is automatically numbered because it has an AutoNumber property set.

InvNum	InvDate	EmpID	CustID
1	12/15/2016	JFW	SmithW
2	12/2/2016	MJW	SantosE
3	1/1/2016	JMM	SantosE
4	11/30/2016	JMM	SmithW

12. Choose **File→Save** or click the **Save** button on the Quick Access toolbar and save the table with the name **`Invoices`**.
13. **Close** [×] the table, but leave the database open.

Creating Tables in Design View

You may find it easier to create a new table in Design View because it offers a straightforward layout and intuitive options for entering field names, setting data types, adding field descriptions, and setting field properties.

Field Properties

Each field data type has numerous properties that can be set to assist with data entry, formatting of displayed data, and other useful functions. Properties are set while working in Design View.

DEVELOP YOUR SKILLS: A1-D4

In this exercise, you will create a new table using Table Design View. Then, you will adjust the width of the table columns.

1. Choose **Create→Tables→Table Design**.

   Access opens an empty table in Design View.

2. Type **CustID** in the Field Name box and tap Tab.
3. Tap Tab to accept *Short Text* as the Data Type.
4. Type **Customer Last Name and First Initial** in the Description field and tap Tab.

   It's a good idea to use field descriptions when setting up tables to help keep track of the purpose and intent of the fields.

5. Click in the **CustID** field and choose **Design→Tools→Primary Key**.

   CustID is now a required field, and each record must have a unique customer ID. Notice the key icon next to the CustID field name, indicating it is the primary key field.

6. Click in the empty box below the CustID field and complete the following fields as shown:

Table1

Field Name	Data Type	Description (Optional)
CustID	Short Text	Customer Last Name and First Initial
CustLastName	Short Text	
CustFirstName	Short Text	
CustStreetAddress	Short Text	
CustCity	Short Text	
CustState	Short Text	2 character state abbreviation
CustZip	Short Text	5 digit ZIP code
CustPhone	Short Text	Area code and number
CustEmail	Hyperlink	
Notes	Long Text	Special comments

7. Click anywhere in the **CustLastName** field, and the Field Properties for that field will display at the bottom of the window.
8. Change the Field Size property to **25** and enter **Last Name** as the Caption property.

   The field will now only accept last names of up to 25 characters in length. The Caption property will make Last Name the label that appears for the field when the table is displayed in Layout View and when the table is used in queries, forms, and reports. Good database design requires the actual field

ACCESS

names follow certain guidelines such as eliminating spaces within the name. The caption lets you follow good design principles while having more descriptive labels for fields.

9. Change the Field Size and Caption properties for the remaining fields as follows:

Field Name	Field Size	Caption
CustFirstName	25	First Name
CustStreetAddress	25	Street
CustCity	15	City
CustState	2	State
CustZIP	5	ZIP
CustPhone	15	Telephone
CustEmail		Email

10. Choose **File→Save** or click the **Save** button on the Quick Access toolbar and save the table as **`Customers`**.

    If you ever forget to save, Access will prompt you to save when you close a table or other object.

    In the next few steps, you will set an input mask property for the CustPhone field. The input mask will automatically format telephone numbers as they are entered, adding parentheses, ( ), around the area code and a hyphen, -, between the digits.

11. Click anywhere in the **CustPhone** field and then click in the **Input Mask** property box.
12. Click the **Input Mask** button on the right side of the property box to display the Input Mask Wizard.

    The Input Mask Wizard has several steps that can be used to fine-tune the mask. However, the default settings will work just fine.

13. Click **Finish** to complete the input mask and apply it to the CustPhone field.
14. Click the **View menu** button ▼, choose **Datasheet View**, and choose **Yes** when asked if you want to save the table.

    Notice the CustID field is still listed as CustID because you did not apply a caption in the preceding steps. However, all other fields now display the captions you entered previously.

    In the next step you will enter records. Notice as you are entering records that the input mask you just created formats the telephone numbers, and the email field is automatically formatted as a hyperlink because of the field type setting you made. Also, feel free to widen the columns slightly by dragging the double-headed arrow between column headings if you need more space to see all the data.

15. Enter the following records.

    Be sure to check your data entry for accuracy.

Customers

CustID	Last Name	First Name	Street	City	State	ZIP	Telephone	Email	Notes
AndersM	Anders	Mark	205 Pine St	Bradenton	FL	34211	(941) 555-2309	MAnders@email.com	
DavisP	Davis	Peter	65 Maple St	Sarasota	FL	34228	(941) 555-1792	PDavis@email.com	
JeffriesD	Jeffries	Daniel	102 Fern St	Bradenton	FL	34209	(941) 555-6939	DannyJ@email.com	

16. Choose **File→Close** to close the database.

Sorting and Filtering Table Data

The primary purpose of any database is to locate and retrieve data quickly and efficiently. Sorting and filtering table records can help accomplish this goal.

When a table is created the records are automatically sorted using the primary key field. This can be changed by applying an ascending or descending sort to other table fields. You can even sort on more than one field so customers could be sorted by last name and then by first name.

Home→Sort & Filter→Ascending *or* Descending

Filtering displays a subset of records. For example, in a customer table you may want to only view customer records for customers that live in a specific zip code. This is accomplished by applying a filter to the zip code field.

Home→Sort & Filter→Filter

DEVELOP YOUR SKILLS: A1-D5

In this exercise, you will sort and filter records in a database for a medical clinic named Raritan Clinic East.

1. Open **A1-D5-RCE** from your **Access Chapter 1** folder and save it as `A1-D5-RCERevised`.

   Enable the content whenever the Security Warning message appears.

Apply a Sort

2. Double-click the **Patients** table in the Navigation pane to open it in **Datasheet View**.

   Notice the records are sorted in ascending order (smallest to largest) on the Patient ID primary key field. Records are always sorted on the primary key field unless a sort is applied to one or more other fields.

3. Click on any name in the Last Name column, and then click the **Ascending** button.

Apply a Filter

4. Double-click the **Raritan Clinic East Doctors** table.
5. Click anywhere in the Zip column and click the **Filter** button.
6. Uncheck the **Select All** box and then check the **34205** box.
7. Click **OK** to apply the filter.

   Just two records should now be visible. The remaining records are still in the table but are hidden from view because of the filter.

8. Close both tables and save the changes.

   The sort and filter you applied will be active next time the tables are used.

9. Choose **File→Close** to close the database.

Importing Data Sources

Organizations frequently have data in text files, Excel worksheets, and other formats that needs to be imported into a database. It's easy to import data into Access using the Import & Link tools. Data is imported into tables that become part of the database. Excel workbooks are the most common source of imported data.

External Data→Import & Link→Excel

DEVELOP YOUR SKILLS: A1-D6

In this exercise, you will import an Excel worksheet into a new table.

1. Open **A1-D6-WinWebDesign** from your **Access Chapter 1** folder and save it as `A1-D6-WinWebDesignRevised`.

   Enable the content whenever the security warning message appears.
2. Click the **External Data** Ribbon tab and notice the available Import & Link options.
3. Choose **Excel** and take a moment to examine the options in the first screen of the Get External Data Wizard.

   You will leave the "how and where" option set to Import the Source Data into a New Table in the Current Database. Notice the data could also be appended (added) to an existing table if desired.
4. Click the **Browse** button and navigate to your **Access Chapter 1** folder, choose **A1-D6-WebContacts**, and click **Open**.
5. Click **OK** to start the import and display the second Wizard screen.
6. Check the **First Row Contains Column Headings** box and click **Next** to specify the Excel column headings as the field names in the new table.

   Notice the next Wizard screens let you adjust various settings, including field names and data types. In the next step you will change the data type for the email field, changing it to a hyperlink.
7. Click in the Email column and click the **Data Type menu** button ▼.
8. Choose **Hyperlink** and click **Next**.

   The new Email field hyperlink formatting won't show up until the import is complete.
9. Click **Next** again to let Access add a primary key field with autonumbering.
10. Name the table `Web Contacts` and click **Finish**.
11. Choose **Close** on the final Wizard screen without checking the Save Import Steps box.

    The Web Contacts table appears at the bottom of the Tables list in the Navigation pane.
12. Double-click the **Web Contacts** table to open it in Datasheet View.

    Notice the hyperlink format is applied to the Email field.
13. Adjust the column widths to fit the widest entries in each column by either dragging the column head borders or autofitting the columns by double-clicking between two column heads.
14. Save the database and save changes to the table if prompted to do so.

Relational Databases

Early database programs stored data in one large, flat file similar to a worksheet. If a sales person sold merchandise and the same product was sold many times, these databases required the sales person to enter the same product description and price for every transaction. Such repetitive data entry is time consuming and bound to cause data errors and inconsistencies.

Relational databases like Access link tables together using primary key fields. A good example is linking a Sales Person table with a Sales Invoices table. One sales person might be linked to hundreds of sales invoices for which they receive commissions. Once a relationship between the Sales Person and Sales Invoices tables is created, all that's needed to associate an invoice with a sales person is to choose the correct sales person when creating the invoice. This type of relationship is called a one-to-many relationship because one sales person is responsible for many invoices. The other types of database relationships are one-to-one and many-to-many, although they are not frequently used.

≡ Database Tools→Relationships→Relationships

Referential Integrity

Referential integrity is an option that can be chosen when creating a relationship between tables. It is a set of rules that prevents changes from being made to fields or records that are related to other fields or records. For example, if referential integrity were in effect, then a salesperson could not be removed from a database that has invoices assigned to that sales person. Referential integrity would require all of the invoices either be removed (not a good idea) or associated with a different sales person before the original sales person's record could be deleted. Referential integrity also requires the data types of related fields to be the same or compatible.

Data Normalization

A properly designed database organizes tables and fields into their smallest usable units and then links them together using relationships. This is known as normalization. Normalization eliminates data duplication, decreases data entry errors and inconsistencies, reduces file size, and streamlines the search for necessary information. An example of reducing fields to their smallest usable units would be to use separate fields for first name and last name rather than a single name field. If a single name field were used, then the database could never be searched or sorted by just last name or first name.

DEVELOP YOUR SKILLS: A1-D7

In this exercise, you will open the Relationships window, add tables, create a one-to-many relationship between the Invoices table and the Employees table, and set referential integrity for the relationship.

1. If necessary, open the **A1-D6-WinWebDesignRevised** database.
2. Choose **Database Tools→Relationships→Relationships**.
3. Click the **Show Table** button.

4. Add the **Employees** and **Invoices** tables to the Relationship window and close the Show Table box.

   The one-to-many relationship between the EmpID fields is automatically created because it is a primary key in the Employees table and a foreign (or secondary) key in the Invoices table. The line connecting the tables is called a join line. There's a 1 on the Employees side of the join line because EmpID is the primary key in that table. EmpID is a foreign key in the Invoices table, so it has an infinity symbol on that side of the join line. Each employee can have an unlimited number of invoices associated with them.

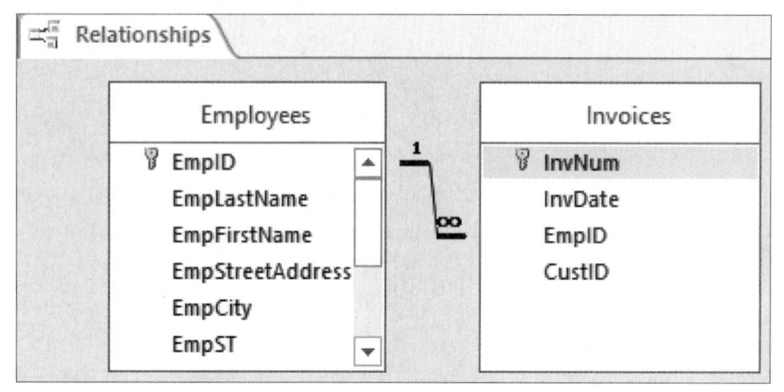

5. Click the **Close** button above the relationship and choose **Yes** to save the relationship.
6. Choose **File→Close** to close the database and then close Access.

Self-Assessment

Check your knowledge of this chapter's key concepts and skills using the Self-Assessment in your ebook or eLab course.

Reinforce Your Skills

REINFORCE YOUR SKILLS: A1-R1

Create a Table in Datasheet View

In this exercise, you will create a new database and a table using Datasheet View.

1. Start Access and choose **Blank Desktop Database** from the template list.
2. Click the **Browse Folders** button and save the database in your **Access Chapter 1** folder as **A1-R1-K4C**.
3. Click the **Create** button to start a new database.
4. Double-click the **ID** heading and change the text to **StID**.

   This will be the primary key field with autonumbering, so your records will automatically get numbered.
5. Tap Tab, choose **Short Text** as the data type, and change the heading from *Field1* to **StLName**.
6. Add **StFName**, **StAdd**, **StCity**, **StST**, **StZIP**, **StPhone**, and **StAvail** as fields with the Short Text data type.
7. Choose **File→Save** or click the **Save** button on the QuickAccess toolbar and save your table as **Staff**.
8. Click the first empty cell in the **StLName** field and enter the following records using these guidelines:
   - Use the Tab key to complete your entries.
   - Enter hyphens in the phone field, as the field is not formatted with an Input Mask.
   - Widen the columns as necessary.
   - Strive for 100% accuracy when entering data, including spaces between characters and uppercase and lowercase letters.

Staff

StID	StLName	StFName	StAdd	StCity	StST	StZIP	StPhone	StAvail
1	Bryant	Matthew	12 Macintosh St	Sarasota	FL	34022	941-555-7523	Thursday
2	Earle	Kevin	77 Kingfisher Ct	Sarasota	FL	34024	941-555-1368	Monday

9. Choose **File→Close** to close the database.

REINFORCE YOUR SKILLS: A1-R2

Create a Table in Design View

In this exercise, you will create a new table using Table Design View. Then, you will adjust the width of the table columns.

1. Choose **File**, create a **Blank Desktop Database**, and save it in your **Access Chapter 1** folder as **A1-R2-K4C**.
2. Click the **Create** button and then switch to **Design View**.
3. Save the table with the name **Children**, and the design grid will appear.
4. Replace the field name *ID* with **ChID** and tap Tab.

   Notice the key icon to the left of the Field Name indicating this is a primary key field.
5. Change the Data Type to **Short Text** and tap Tab.

ACCESS

6. Type **Last Name and First Initial** and tap Tab to complete the description.
7. Enter the remaining fields shown here using the data types and descriptions shown:

Children

Field Name	Data Type	Description (Optional)
ChID	Short Text	Last Name and First Initial
ChLName	Short Text	
ChFName	Short Text	
ChAdd	Short Text	
ChCity	Short Text	
ChST	Short Text	2-char abbreviation
ChZIP	Short Text	5-digit ZIP code
ChPhone	Short Text	Area code & number
ChBday	Date/Time	

8. Click anywhere in the **ChPhone** field and then click in the **Input Mask** property box.
9. Click the **Input Mask** button on the right side of the Input Mask property box and choose **Yes** if asked to save the table.
10. Click **Finish** to accept the Phone Number input mask and apply it to the ChPhone field.
11. Switch to **Datasheet View**, saving the table if prompted to do so.
12. Enter the following records, adjusting the column widths as necessary:

Children

ChID	ChLName	ChFName	ChAdd	ChCity	ChST	ChZIP	ChPhone	ChBday
CregerK	Creger	Kurt	503 Hillview St	Sarasota	FL	34022	(941) 555-0245	10/12/2001
LangfordJ	Langford	James	43 Wisteria Ct	Bradenton	FL	34209	(941) 555-1098	8/13/2000

13. Choose **File→Close** to close the database, and save the changes if prompted to do so.

REINFORCE YOUR SKILLS: A1-R3

Create, Import, and Sort Tables and Establish Relationships

The staff director of Kids for Change would like you to add two new tables to the database: one that stores various community activities and one that stores parent volunteers. You'll create one of these tables and import the other.

1. Open **A1-R3-K4C** from your **Access Chapter 1** folder and save it as **A1-R3-K4CRevised**.

Import an Excel Worksheet

The first thing you'll do is import a worksheet into a table, which will then be linked with other tables through relationships.

2. Choose **External Data→Import & Link→Excel**.
3. Click the **Browse** button on the first Wizard screen and navigate to your **Access Chapter 1** folder.
4. Choose **A1-R3-ActivityParticipation** and click **Open**.
5. Click **OK** to import the worksheet into a new table and display the next Wizard screen.
6. Click **Next** again to choose **ActivityParticipation** as the worksheet to use.
7. Check the **First Row Contains Column Headings** box and click **Next** to specify the Excel column headings as the field names in the new table.

8. Click **Next** again to accept the data type of the two fields as Short Text.
9. Click **Next** again to let Access add a primary key field.
10. Click **Finish** to accept ActivityParticipation as the table name and then click **Close** to complete the import.

    ActivityParticipation *should now be in the table list.*

Sort the Imported Worksheet

11. Double-click the **ActivityParticipation** table to open it in Datasheet View.

    Notice the table is sorted in ascending order by Activity ID.

12. Click anywhere in the **Child ID** column and choose **Home→Sort & Filter→Ascending**.

    The records are now sorted by Child ID to easily see all the activities each child has participated in.

13. Close the table and save the changes.

Create Relationships

14. Choose **Database Tools→Relationships→Relationships**.

    Notice there is currently a relationship between the Donors and Donations tables.

15. Click the **Show Table** button.
16. Add the **Children**, **ActivityParticipation**, and **Activities** tables, and then close the Show Table box.
17. Drag the **Child ID** primary key field from the Children table and drop it on the ChildID field in the Activity Participation table.

    Make sure ChildID appears in both the Table/Query and Related Table/Query lists.

18. Check the **Enforce Referential Integrity** box and then click the **Create** button to complete the relationship.
19. Drag the **ActID** field from the Activities table and drop it on the ActID field in the **ActivityParticipation** table.
20. Choose to **Enforce Referential Integrity** and then click **Create**.

    These relationships will now allow a database user to determine all the activities a particular child has participated in and to view the details of those activities.

21. Click the **Close** button above the relationships and choose **Yes** to save the relationships.

Add a Table in Design View

22. Choose **Create→Tables→Table**.
23. Choose **Home →Views→Design View** and save the table as `Volunteers`.
24. Follow these guidelines to set up the table and enter a record:
    - Let VolID be the primary key field with autonumbering.
    - Set the data type of all fields (except the primary key field) to **Short Text**.
    - Enter the one record shown here, keying in the hyphens in the phone number:

Volunteers

VolID	VolLName	VolFName	VolStreet	VolCity	VolST	VolZIP	VolPhone	AvailDay
1	Jones	Stan	892 South St	Sarasota	FL	34024	941-555-8929	Tuesday

25. Choose **File→Close** when you are finished. Save the changes if prompted to do so.

ACCESS

Apply Your Skills

APPLY YOUR SKILLS: A1-A1

Create a Database and Tables

In this exercise, you will create a new database with two tables.

1. Create a new database and save it to your **Access Chapter 1** folder as **`A1-A1-SunStateU`**.
2. Create a new table named **`Classes`** using the following fields, data types, and captions:

Field	Data Type	Caption
ClassID	Short Text (Primary Key)	
Department	Short Text	
ClassNumber	Short Text	Class Number
SectionNumber	Short Text	Section Number
RoomNumber	Short Text	Room Number
StartTime	Date/Time	Start Time
EndTime	Date/Time	End Time
CreditHours	Number	Credit Hours

3. Brainstorm and add at least two records to the table.
4. Close the table when you have finished adding records.
5. Create another new table named **`Professors`**, using the following fields and data types and making **ProfID** the primary key field:

Field Name	Data Type
ProfID	Short Text
ProfLastName	Short Text
ProfFirstName	Short Text
ProfDept	Short Text
ProfRank	Short Text

6. Brainstorm and add at least two new records to the table.
7. Close the table when you have finished adding records.
8. Choose **File→Close** to close the database.

APPLY YOUR SKILLS: A1-A2

Import a Table and Establish a Relationship

In this exercise, you will import an Excel worksheet and establish a relationship between the new table and a currently existing table.

1. Open **A1-A2-Customers** from your **Access Chapter 1** folder and save it as **`A1-A2-CustomersRevised`**.
2. Open the **Customers** table in **Datasheet View**.
3. Sort the records in **Ascending** order on the **CustZIP** field.

4. Widen all columns to fit the widest entry in the columns.
5. Close the table, saving the changes.

Import a Worksheet

6. Follow these guidelines to import the **A1-A2-Invoices** workbook (located in your **Access Chapter 1** folder) as a table into the open database:
   - Leave all field names and data types as they are in the Wizard.
   - Make **InvNum** the primary key field.
   - Save the table as `Invoices`.
7. Double-click the **Invoices** table to open it in Datasheet View.
8. Sort the table in **Ascending** order on the **EmpID** field.
9. Close the table, saving the changes.

Establish a Relationship

10. Open the **Relationships** window and create a relationship between the CustID fields in the Customers and Invoices tables, enforcing referential integrity.
11. Close the Relationships window and save the changes to the relationship.
12. Choose **File→Close** to close the database.

APPLY YOUR SKILLS: A1-A3

Create a Table, Import a Database, and Establish a Relationship

In this exercise, you will create a database to track the courses taught by specific teachers in a nonprofit organization.

1. Create a new database and save it to your **Access Chapter 1** folder as `A1-A3-Teachers`.
2. Follow these guidelines to create the table below:
   - Use the table name, field names, and data shown here.
   - Set all data types to **Short Text** and make **TeacherID** the primary key field.
   - Enter the data shown:

Teachers

TeacherID	TFirstName	TLastName	TStatus
Amack	Alex	Mack	Fulltime
Bsmith	Brian	Smith	Parttime
Jjones	Jack	Jones	Parttime
Twatts	Tonya	Watts	Fulltime

3. Close the table and save it with the name `Teachers`, if prompted to do so.
4. Import the Excel workbook named **A1-A3-Courses** from your **Access Chapter 1** folder using **CourseID** as the primary key field, and name the table `Courses`.
5. Establish a one-to-many relationship between the **TeacherID** fields in the **Teachers** and **Courses** tables, and enforce referential integrity.
6. Close and save the Relationships window and close the database.

Extend Your Skills

These exercises challenge you to think critically and apply your new skills. You will be evaluated on your ability to follow directions, completeness, creativity, and the use of proper grammar and mechanics. Save files to your chapter folder. Submit assignments as directed.

A1-E1 That's the Way I See It

You've volunteered to help a nonprofit organization determine how much recyclable material is being collected by the five recycling centers in the area. You've been tasked with creating a database with contact information for the five centers. You are also tasked with visiting the five centers, gathering information on the recyclables they accept and the annual number of metric tons of each that they've collected each year over the past three years. The annual tonnage information needs to be in a separate table that is related to the Centers table. Save your completed database as **A1-E1-Recycle**.

A1-E2 Be Your Own Boss

You are the owner of Blue Jean Landscaping and have decided to sponsor the Sarasota Service Guild, a nonprofit organization created to raise money to help adults with disabilities. They need a database that tracks businesses that donate to the guild and the donations that are made. Create a database with tables and fields to track the businesses and the donations they make. Create a relationship that can be used to relate businesses to the donations they've made over the past five years. Populate your tables with information for two businesses, with each making an annual donation over the past five years. Include relevant information about the businesses, including their names, addresses, and primary contact information. Include the amount and date of the annual donations. Save your completed database as **A1-E2-BJL**.

A1-E3 Demonstrate Proficiency

Stormy BBQ wants to modernize its business. They have hired you to design and create a database for their BBQ restaurant. Use Access to create a database with three tables: one for staff, one for menu items, and one for transactions where each transaction lists the menu items on that transaction including the quantity and price of each item. Relate the menu and transactions tables. Enter enough data to be able to view and modify the tables as needed. Save your completed database as **A1-E3-StormyBBQ**.

ACCESS

2 Working with Forms

In this chapter, you will create and use forms. If you have ever entered your personal information on a college application, filled out a loan application, or purchased an item from an online retailer, you have used a form. You also use forms to sign up for Facebook, Flickr, and Gmail accounts. A form ideally provides an attractive and easy-to-use interface, which allows a user to focus on one table record at a time.

LEARNING OBJECTIVES

- Create basic forms
- Create forms using the Forms Wizard
- Modify forms using Layout View
- Modify forms using Design View
- Set properties for form sections and form controls
- Set the tab order of a form
- Create multiple item forms and split forms

Project: Designing Forms at Winchester Web Design

As the information technology (IT) director at Winchester Web Design, you are responsible for designing and formatting the forms and reports in the company database to make them more attractive, consistent, and user friendly. Part of your job is to customize forms so they better identify the company. To accomplish this, you plan to create a consistent color scheme and add the corporate name and logo to all the company's forms.

Creating Forms

A form is a database object used to enter, edit, or view the data for individual table records. Forms are a nice alternative to the row and column arrangement of table Datasheet View. Being able to view and focus on a single record can help ensure data accuracy.

Record Sources

Forms display data from a record source, which is typically a single table or query. However, if a relationship exists between two or more tables, fields from all related tables can be displayed on the same form. An example is an Invoice form that displays data from the Invoice, Products, Customers, and Employee tables.

Invoices

Winchester Web Design
Invoices

Invoice Number 1
Invoice Date 2 /15/2016
Customer ID SmithW
Employee ID JFW
Last Name Smith
Emp Last Name Winchester
First Name William
Emp First Name Jay
Street Address 879 Fifteenth Ave
City Bradenton
State FL ZIP 34210
Telephone (941) 555-0793
Email SmithBilly@email.com

ProdID	Description	Price	Qty	Line Total
01HP	Home Page, Nav, CSS, Design	$400.00	4	$1,600.00
02SP	Secondary Page	$200.00	1	$200.00
05IM	Image, Custom Designed	$40.00	2	$80.00
*				

Record: 4 of 4 No Filter Search

A form with fields from the Invoice, Products, Customers, and Employee tables

Creating and Using Basic Forms

Use the Form button to instantly create a basic form for a selected table or query. This is the easiest way to create a form using all fields from the table or query. Only one table or query can be used in a basic form.

Create→Forms→Form

DEVELOP YOUR SKILLS: A2-D1

In this exercise, you will create a basic form and edit a record using the form.

1. Open **A2-D1-WinWebDesign** from your **Access Chapter 2** folder and save it as **A2-D1-WinWebDesignRevised**.

   When completing exercises, always choose to Enable Content.

2. Choose the **Employee Spouses** table in the Navigation pane by clicking the table name (don't double-click).
3. Choose **Create→Forms→Form**.

   A basic form based on the Employee Spouses table is displayed in Layout View. Layout View is used to size and position form controls.

4. Close any boxes that may be open, such as the Property Sheet or Field List box.
5. Click the **View menu** button ▼ and choose **Form View**.

   Form View is used for entering, editing, and viewing table records one at a time.

6. Use the navigation controls at the bottom of the form to browse the records from the underlying table.

   Record: |◀ ◀ 1 of 3 ▶ ▶| ▶* No Filter Search

7. Navigate to record 2 (the Tom Franklin record) and change the last four digits of the phone number to **6767**.
8. Choose **File→Save** or click the **Save** button on the Quick Access toolbar and save the form as **Employee Spouses**.
9. Click the **Close** × button on the right side of the form.

Creating Forms with the Form Wizard

The Form Wizard is a great way to get started with the creation of most forms. It lets you choose the fields you want from one or more tables or queries (the data source) and then builds a form from the chosen fields. The form can then easily be modified using Layout View or Design View.

Create→Forms→Form Wizard

DEVELOP YOUR SKILLS: A2-D2

In this exercise, you will use the Form Wizard to create a form.

1. If necessary, open the **A2-D1-WinWebDesignRevised** database.
2. Choose the **Customers** table in the Navigation pane.

3. Choose **Create→Forms→Form Wizard**.

   Customers is chosen in the Tables/Queries list because you chose it prior to starting the Wizard.

4. Click the **Add All Fields** >> button and click **Next**.

   This adds all fields from the Customers table to the Selected Fields list. You could add fields from other tables and queries as well, although you won't do that now.

5. Click **Next** again to accept the Columnar layout format.
6. Leave the form name as *Customers* and click **Finish**.

   The form is displayed in Form View and is ready for data entry or editing.

Changing Forms in Layout View

A typical form has a header section where tiles, logos, and decorative elements are displayed and a detail section with text boxes and labels where data is displayed. These objects can easily be sized, moved, edited, and removed in Layout View. Multiple objects can be changed together by holding the Ctrl key while selecting them with single mouse clicks.

View the video "Reorganizing Forms in Layout View."

Home→Views→Layout View

DEVELOP YOUR SKILLS: A2-D3

In this exercise, you will size, position, and edit controls, and you'll get extensive practice selecting multiple controls.

1. If necessary, open the **A2-D1-WinWebDesignRevised** database and open the **Customers** form.
2. Click the **View menu** button ▾ and choose **Layout View**.

Edit Labels

3. Click on the **Street Address** label to select it.
4. Click inside the selected label just to the right of *Address*.
5. Use the Backspace key and any other keys as necessary to remove the word *Address*.

   The label should now be Street.

6. Change the *ST* label to `State`.
7. Change the *ZIP* label to `Zip`.

Size Text Boxes

8. Click on the large, empty **Notes** text box (not the label) to select it.
9. Hover the mouse pointer over the right edge until the adjust pointer appears.

10. Drag left, reducing the box width to equal the Email text box width.

11. Reduce the width of the State text box so it is slightly wider than the two-character state abbreviation.

Change the Position of Labels and Text Boxes

In the next few steps, you will move the text boxes so they are closer to the labels.

12. Click the large **Notes** text box.
13. Press and hold Crtl and click the **Email** text box.

    Both boxes should be selected.
14. Press and hold Ctrl while you select all other text boxes in the column.

    Use Undo if you accidentally move the boxes while selecting.
15. Tap the **left arrow** ← key repeatedly to move the text boxes closer to the labels.

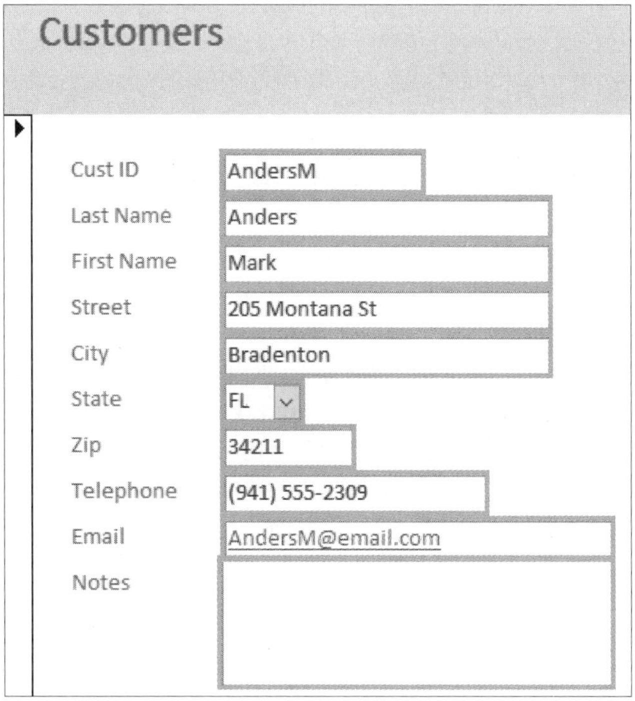

16. Click an empty part of the form to deselect all boxes.
17. Use the mouse and Ctrl key to select the **Telephone**, **Email**, and **Notes** labels and text boxes.

18. Use the keyboard or drag with your mouse (when the four-headed arrow appears) to move the labels and text boxes up and right as shown here.

Customers

Customers

Cust ID AndersM
Last Name Anders
First Name Mark
Street 205 Montana St
City Bradenton
State FL
Zip 34211
Telephone (941) 555-2309
Email AndersM@email.com
Notes

19. Make any additional adjustments to the controls you deem necessary.
20. Choose **File→Save** or click the **Save** button on the Quick Access toolbar to save the changes to the form.

Changing Forms in Design View

Form Layout View is a great tool for editing, sizing, and rearranging labels and text boxes, but there are many form design details that can be more precisely set using Design View. In Design View you can precisely control any part of a form and its controls. The Property Sheet is used in both Layout View and Design View to specify the details for any form object.

Design→Views→Design View

Design→Tools→Property Sheet

Modify the Form Header Section

The Form Header and Footer appear at the top and bottom of the form. The Form Header typically has one or more titles and often a logo and decorative features. Form Footers are rarely used. The Form Header can be modified in either Layout View or Design View.

DEVELOP YOUR SKILLS: A2-D4

In this exercise, you will format the Form Header and field labels and insert a logo to make the form look more professional.

1. If necessary, open the **A2-D1-WinWebDesignRevised** database and open the **Customers** form.
2. Choose **Design→Views→Design View**.

   Notice the Form Header contains the Customers title and the text boxes and their labels are located in the Detail section.

Set Properties for the Form Title

3. Click inside the **Customers** title box in the Form Header and change the title to `Winchester Customers`.

   Next you will use the Property Sheet to precisely size, position, and format the title.

4. Choose **Design→Tools→Property Sheet**.

   The Property Sheet shows the settings for the currently selected object (the Customers title box).

5. Click in the **Width** box in the Property Sheet and set the Width to `5.5`.

   The setting won't take effect until you click out of the Width box in the next step.

6. Click in the **Left** box and set the Left position to `1.5`.
7. Set the Font Size to **30** and the Font Name to **Lucida Calligraphy**.
8. Choose **Home→Text Formatting→Font Color menu button ▾** and choose a blue color of your choice.

   You can set text formats in this manner or directly in the Property Sheet, if desired.

Set Control Properties in the Detail Section

9. Click the **Cust ID** label (not the text box) in the Detail section and notice the name *CustID_Label* appears at the top of the Property Sheet.

   The Property Sheet always indicates which control is currently selected. Next you will select all labels in the Detail section. Properties can be set for multiple controls at the same time, provided the controls are of the same type (labels or text boxes).

   Property Sheet
   Selection type: Label
   CustID_Label

10. Press and hold the Ctrl key and click all labels in the Detail section to select them all.

    Notice in the Property Sheet that many properties like Width and Height are identical for all labels. Other properties like Top and Left positioning are blank because they are not the same for all labels.

11. Apply the same blue font color that you just applied to the title.

Insert a Logo

12. Choose **Design→Header/Footer→Logo**.

13. Navigate to your **Access Chapter 2** folder, choose **WWD-Logo.bmp**, and click **OK**.

    Access places the logo in the upper-left corner of the Report Header section, but it's a bit small. The logo should be selected so the Property Sheet will show the logo properties.

14. Set both the Width and Height properties to `0.8`.

    The Form Header will increase in height slightly to accommodate the logo.

15. Switch to **Form View** to see the changes.

Explore Property Sheets for Sections and the Form

16. Switch to **Design View**.
17. Click the **Form Header** section bar and view the Property Sheet.

    The Property Sheet should be set to FormHeader. Notice you can specify the width and height of the header area and set formats like the background color.

18. Click the **Detail** section bar and examine its properties.
19. Click the **Selection Type menu** button ▼ in the Property Sheet, scroll through the list, and choose **Form**.

    The Form properties control the overall appearance and functionality of the form. Properties for the form can also be accessed by clicking the Select Form box at the top-left corner of the form as shown here.

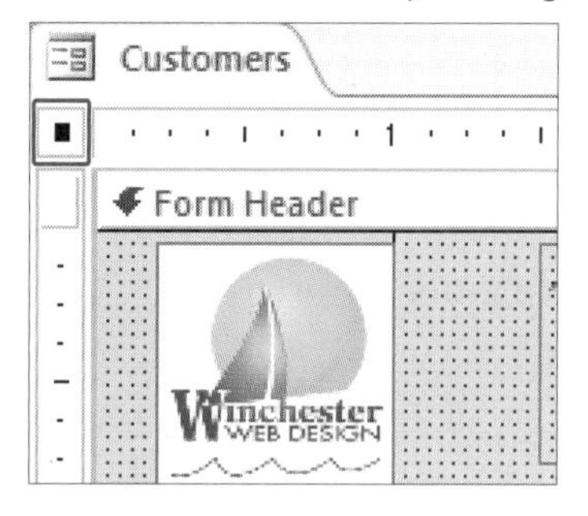

Tab Order

The most effective way to enter a record using a form is to tap the Tab key to move from one field to the next. Forms have a tab order that determines which field the insertion point moves to each time the Tab key is tapped. The tab order can be changed to allow fields to be entered in a different sequence. This may be necessary if fields are rearranged on a form and when fields from more than one table appear on the same form.

Design→Tools→Tab Order

DEVELOP YOUR SKILLS: A2-D5

In this exercise, you will change the form tab order to make the telephone number the second field in the tab order.

1. Switch to **Form View**.
2. Use the Tab key to cycle through the fields.

    Notice that the last name field is the first field in the tab order after the CustID field.

3. Switch to **Design View**.

4. Choose **Design→Tools→Tab Order**.
5. Follow these steps to adjust the tab order:

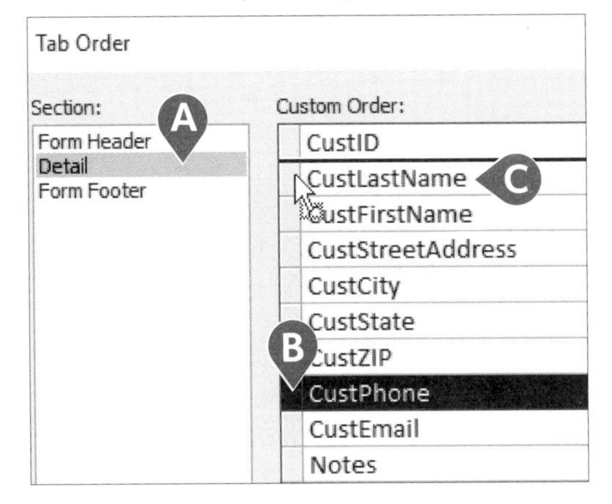

   A. Choose **Detail** to see the current tab order for fields in the Detail section.
   B. Click the small selection box next to the CustPhone field.
   C. Drag the **CustPhone** selection box up and drop it above the CustLastName field. CustPhone should now be second in the tab order.

6. Click **OK** to complete the tab order change.
7. Switch to **Form View** and tap [Tab] repeatedly to cycle through the fields.

   The tab order remains the same with the exception of Telephone, which is now the second field in the order.

Themes

Themes are prepackaged groups of design elements such as background colors, font families, font sizes, and other properties. When themes are applied, they impact all objects in the database (tables, forms, queries, and reports). The Themes group on the Ribbon lets you change just the colors or fonts, or the overall design including both the colors and fonts.

Design→Themes→Themes

DEVELOP YOUR SKILLS: A2-D6

In this exercise, you will apply a theme to your form.

1. Switch to **Design View** and choose **Design→Themes→Themes**.
2. Hover over each theme's thumbnail and notice how the form changes.

   Access themes are subtle, applying small, incremental changes to the form. Keep in mind that themes are applied to all objects in the database (tables, forms, queries, and reports). And once a theme is applied, it cannot be undone.

3. Choose your favorite **theme** and then switch to **Form View** to see how your finished form looks with the new theme.
4. If desired, switch back to **Design View** and choose a different **theme** or switch to **Layout View** to change the position and size of controls on your form.
5. Close your form, saving the changes, if prompted to do so.

Creating Other Types of Forms

A typical large organization will have a need for many types of forms. Different departments within an organization may need to access the same database tables but may need to view different fields from within those tables. A good example would be the difference between what a customer service representative and a sales person might need. They will both have a need to access customer information, but the sales person will also want to see sales history, sales opportunities, and other information that a customer service representative won't need. Large organizations typically have an extensive collection of forms designed to make their staff highly efficient.

Creating Multiple Item Forms

Most forms are designed to let the user focus on one record at a time. Sometimes, however, it is necessary to print multiple items in a table using a layout that is more appropriate for printing and distributing than a table datasheet. The multiple item form is used for those occasions.

Multiple item forms resemble datasheets because data appears in rows and columns. However, multiple item forms can be customized to enhance the appearance of the form using colors, graphics, and other design elements.

Create→Forms→More Forms→Multiple Items

DEVELOP YOUR SKILLS: A2-D7

In this exercise, you will create a multiple item form.

1. If necessary, open the **A2-D1-WinWebDesignRevised** database.
2. Choose the **Customers** table in the Navigation pane.
3. Choose **Create→Forms→More Forms→Multiple Items**.

   Notice the datasheet-like appearance of the form.
4. Choose **Design→Themes→Themes** and choose a theme that has text sizes and formatting you like.
5. If necessary, click on any of the customer IDs in the CustID column to select all cells in that column.

   The selected cells will have faint yellow borders.
6. Drag the right border of the selected cells to the left, reducing the column width.
7. Reduce all column widths to see if you can get the form to fit on your screen.

8. Click the **Forms** icon in the form header next to the Customers title and tap Delete to remove it.

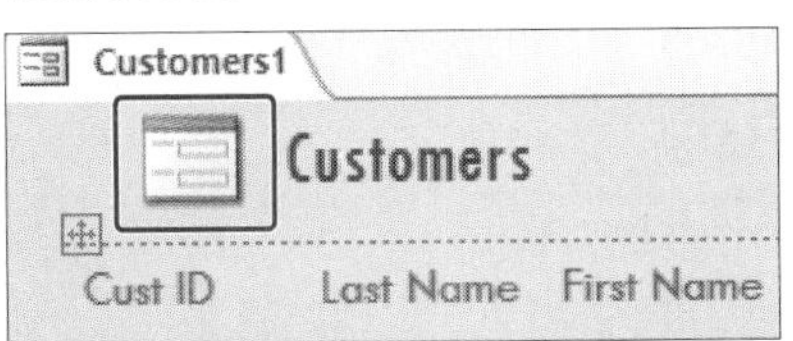

Your completed form is now ready to be used as an alternative to a datasheet for data entry and other uses.

9. Close the form and save it as **`CustomersMultiItem`**.

Creating Split Forms

A split form simultaneously shows a table in Datasheet View and a form displaying a single record from the table. The views are synchronized so that a selected record in one view is also selected in the other view.

Create→Forms→More Forms→Split Form

DEVELOP YOUR SKILLS: A2-D8

In this exercise, you will create a split form.

1. Choose the **Customers** table in the Navigation pane.
2. Choose **Create→Forms→More Forms→Split Form**.

   Click any record in the datasheet and notice that it displays in the form.
3. The form is displayed in Layout View, so adjust the field widths in the form and the datasheet as needed.
4. Remove the Forms icon that is next to the Customers heading.
5. Choose **File→Close** to close the database and save the form as **`CustomersSplitForm`**.

Self-Assessment

Check your knowledge of this chapter's key concepts and skills using the Self-Assessment in your ebook or eLab course.

Reinforce Your Skills

REINFORCE YOUR SKILLS: A2-R1

Create a Form Using the Form Wizard and Then Customize It

Kids for Change has hired you to create a new form and customize it with a new design. In this exercise, you will use the Form Wizard to create a form, add an image, and set several formatting properties.

1. Open **A2-R1-K4C** from your **Access Chapter 2** folder and save it as **`A2-R1-K4CRevised`**.
   Enable the content when prompted.

Create a Form Using the Form Wizard

2. Choose the **Children** table in the Navigation pane.
3. Choose **Create→Forms→Form Wizard**.
4. Add all fields from the Children table to the Selected Fields list and click **Next**.
5. Keep the **Columnar** layout and click **Next**.
6. Name the form **`Kids for Change Children Volunteers`** and click **Finish**.

Edit and Format the Title

7. Switch to **Design View**.
8. Click inside the title box and position the insertion point just in front of the letter *C* in Children.
9. Press and hold the [Shift] key and tap [Enter] to force *Children Volunteers* to a new line.
10. If necessary, display the **Property Sheet**.
11. Set the following properties for the title.

Property	New Value
Width	3
Font Name	Arial
Font Size	18
Text Align	Center
Font Weight	Semi-bold

Insert a Logo and Set Properties

12. Choose **Design→Header/Footer→Logo**.
13. Navigate to your **Access Chapter 2** folder, choose **K4C-Logo.bmp**, and click **OK**.
14. Set both the Width and Height properties to **`0.7`** and the Left property to **`3.3`**.

Format Text Boxes and Labels

15. Click the **Child ID** label in the Detail section.
16. Press and hold [Ctrl] while you select all other labels.

17. Set the following properties for the labels.

Property	New Value
Width	1.5
Height	0.25
Special Effect	Raised
Font Name	Arial
Font Weight	Semi-bold

18. Select all text boxes in the Detail section and set these properties.

Property	New Value
Height	0.25
Font Name	Arial
Font Weight	Semi-bold

19. Choose **Design→Themes→Themes** and apply the theme of your choice.
20. Switch to **Form View** to see your completed form.
21. Choose **File→Close** to close the database and save the changes to your form.

REINFORCE YOUR SKILLS: A2-R2

Create a Multiple Item Form and Apply a Theme

Kids for Change has hired you to redesign their database forms and apply a consistent and attractive theme to both new and existing forms. In this exercise, you will create a multiple item form for entering and managing staff information. Then you will apply a theme to the new form.

1. Open **A2-R2-K4C** from your **Access Chapter 2** folder and save it as **`A2-R2-K4CRevised`**.
2. Choose the **Staff** table in the Navigation pane and choose **Create→Forms→More Forms→Multiple Items**.
3. Change the title to **`Kids for Change Staff`**.
4. Delete the small image that is just to the left of the *Kids for Change Staff* title.
5. Choose **Design→Themes→Themes** and apply the theme of your choice.
6. Reduce the widths of all columns to fit the widest entries in the columns.
7. Switch to **Form View** to see your completed form.
8. Choose **File→Close** to close the database, saving your form as **`Staff-MultiItem`**.

REINFORCE YOUR SKILLS: A2-R3

Create a Form and Add a Title and an Image

In this exercise, you will create a form to help facilitate the management of the Kids for Change Activities table.

1. Open **A2-R3-K4C** from your **Access Chapter 2** folder and save it as **`A2-R3-K4CRevised`**.

Create a Form and Arrange Controls

2. Use the Form Wizard to create a form from the **Activities** table using all fields in the table, choose the **Columnar** layout, and save the form as `Activities Form`.
3. Switch to **Layout View** and change the title to `Kids for Change Activities`.
4. Widen the title box so the text doesn't wrap inside the box.

   You may need to click outside of the title box and then click on the title again prior to sizing it.
5. Reduce the widths of all labels so they are just slightly wider than the label text.
6. Use the form to navigate through the ten records and reduce the width of the text boxes to be slightly wider than the widest entries.
7. Move the text boxes closer to the labels.
8. Move the **Day of Week** and **Meet Time** labels and text boxes. Add a little extra space between all rows as shown here.

9. Choose **Design→Header/Footer→Logo**.
10. Navigate to your **Access Chapter 2** folder, choose **K4C-Logo.bmp**, and click **OK**.
11. Set both the Width and Height properties to `0.7` and the Left property to `3.6`.
12. Reduce the height of the title box so it's just high enough to hold the title and then move it down in the Form Header so it is vertically centered in the header area as shown here.

13. Choose **Design→Themes→Themes** and apply the theme of your choice.

    If you apply a theme that increases the text size, you may need to go back and adjust the controls' sizes again.
14. Choose **File→Close** to close the database, saving the changes you made to the form.

Apply Your Skills

APPLY YOUR SKILLS: A2-A1

Create and Modify a Form

Universal Corporate Events is a planner of corporate and professional events. You have been tasked with revamping the image of Universal Corp, including everything from reports to forms. In this exercise, you will create a new Personnel form.

1. Open **A2-A1-UniversalCorp** from your **Access Chapter 2** folder and save it as `A2-A1-UniversalCorpRevised`.

Create a Form and Modify the Header Section

2. Use the **Form Wizard** to create a form using all fields from the **Personnel** table, choose the **Columnar** layout, and save the form as `Personnel Mgmt`.
3. Switch to **Layout View** and display the Property Sheet.
4. Click in the title box and set the following properties for the title.

Property	New Value
Width	4
Left	1.5
Text Align	Center

5. Edit the title, creating a two-line title with `Universal Corporate Events Ltd.` on the first line and `Personnel` on the second.

   Remember to use the Ctrl + Enter *keystroke combination to push Personnel to the second line.*
6. Insert **UCE-Logo.bmp**, located in your **Access Chapter 2** folder.
7. Set both the Width and Height properties to `0.7`.

Modify the Detail Section

8. Apply the theme of your choice to the form.
9. Set the Width property of all labels to `1.2`.
10. Set the Width property of the **EmpID**, **ST**, and **Zip** text boxes to `0.6`.
11. Set the Width property of the **First Name**, **Last Name**, **Address**, and **City** text boxes to `1.5`.
12. Set the Width property of the **Email Address** and **Salary Grade** text boxes to `2`.
13. Select all text boxes and move them closer to the labels.
14. Reposition the **Telephone**, **Email Address**, **Date Hired**, and **Salary Grade** labels and text boxes up and to the right of the other fields, creating a two-column form.
15. Switch to **Design View** and change the tab order, making **EmpPhone** the second field in sequence and leaving the rest of the tab order as it currently is.
16. Switch to **Form View** to view the database and test the tab order.
17. When you are finished, close the database, saving the changes you've made to the form.

APPLY YOUR SKILLS: A2-A2

Edit and Format Labels and Text Boxes

In this exercise, you will create a new Personnel form.

1. Open **A2-A2-UniversalCorp** from your **Access Chapter 2** folder and save it as **A2-A2-UniversalCorpRevised**.

Format Controls

2. Open the **Event Schedules** form and switch to **Layout View**.
3. Change the *Location* label to **Venue**.
4. Change the *Event ID* label to **Event Code**.
5. Add **Ltd.** to the title, making it *Universal Corporate Events Ltd.*
6. Display the Property Sheet and change the properties for the Universal Corporate Events Ltd. title as follows.

Property	New Value
Width	4.5
Height	0.3
Font Name	Georgia

7. Set these properties for the Scheduling subtitle.

Property	New Value
Width	4.5
Height	0.3
Font Name	Georgia
Font Weight	Light

8. Select all the labels in the Detail section and set these properties.

Property	New Value
Width	1.3
Height	0.3
Font Name	Arial
Font Size	12
Font Weight	Semi-bold

9. Select all the text boxes in the Detail section and set these properties.

Property	New Value
Height	0.3
Left	1.5
Font Name	Arial
Font Size	14

10. Apply the theme of your choice.

11. Switch to **Form View** to see your completed form.
12. Make any changes to the form, as needed.
13. Close the database, saving the changes to the form.

APPLY YOUR SKILLS: A2-A3

Create a Form, Work with Form Headers, and Add a Logo

In this exercise, you will create a new form for managing UCE's event venue information, add and format a Form Header and title, and add an original company logo.

1. Open **A2-A3-UniversalCorp** from your **Access Chapter 2** folder and save it as `A2-A3-UniversalCorpRevised`.
2. Use the **Form Wizard** to create a form using all fields from the **Venues** table, choose the **Columnar** layout, and save the form as `Event Venues`.
3. Switch to **Layout View** and display the Property Sheet.
4. Click in the title box and set the following properties.

Property	New Value
Height	0.35
Top	0.25
Left	1.5
Font Name	Georgia

5. Insert the **UCE-Logo.bmp** logo, which is located in your **Access Chapter 2** folder.
6. Set the Width and Height properties of the logo to `0.8`.
7. Select all the labels in the Detail section and set these properties.

Property	New Value
Width	1.5
Height	0.25
Font Name	Arial
Font Size	12
Font Weight	Semi-bold

8. Select all the text boxes in the Detail section and set these properties.

Property	New Value
Height	0.25
Left	1.6
Font Name	Arial
Font Size	12

9. Apply the theme of your choice.
10. Switch to **Form View** to see your completed form.
11. If necessary, switch to **Layout View** or **Design View** to make additional changes to the form.
12. Choose **File→Close** to close the database, saving any changes to your form.

Extend Your Skills

These exercises challenge you to think critically and apply your new skills. You will be evaluated on your ability to follow directions, completeness, creativity, and the use of proper grammar and mechanics. Save files to your chapter folder. Submit assignments as directed.

A2-E1 That's the Way I See It

You've been asked to create a sales invoice form for Blue Jean Landscaping that shows all fields from the Sales Invoices query. Open **A2-E1-BJL** and create a well-designed form that is based on the Sales Invoices query and include a title and logo (use **BJL-Logo.bmp**). Make sure all fields are appropriately positioned and sized using the largest entries in the database as a guideline for determining the appropriate text box sizing. Apply a theme of your choice. Save your form as **`Sales Invoices`**.

A2-E2 Be Your Own Boss

Blue Jean Landscaping wants a split form that's based on the Services table. The split form should include all fields from the table, a company logo, and the company name in the Form Header along with a Landscape Services subtitle. Open **A2-E2-BJL** and use the logo **BJL-Logo.bmp**. Make sure all fields are appropriately positioned and sized using the largest entries in the database as a guideline for determining the appropriate text box sizing. Apply a theme of your choice. Save your form as **`Services Split Form`**.

A2-E3 Demonstrate Proficiency

You've been asked by the management of Stormy BBQ, a local BBQ restaurant, to create consistent forms and reports. Open the **A2-E3-StormyBBQ** database and examine the Merchandise form. Create a new form from the Restaurants table that closely matches the Merchandise form. Replicate the layout and formatting of fields and of the Form Header. You may not be able to create a perfect match but try to get the layout and formatting as close to the Merchandise form as possible. Use the **SBQ-Logo.bmp** file and name your new form **`Restaurants`**.

ACCESS

3 Querying a Database

One of the main goals of a database is to organize data so that information can be located and retrieved quickly. People in all types of businesses retrieve stored data and information daily, often at a moment's notice. In this chapter, you will search information that is stored in tables in a relational database and extract records that meet specific criteria using a query, a database object used to locate records based on the conditions you set.

LEARNING OBJECTIVES

- Create, save, and run select queries
- Create select queries using multiple tables
- Use simple query criteria
- Use AND and OR criteria in queries
- Use wildcard characters in query criteria
- Sort query results
- Create and format a calculated field

Project: Using Queries to Get Answers

You have been asked to query the Winchester Web Design database and compile two separate customer lists. The lists will be used to notify all past clients of updates to their website contact forms. The first list will include only the first and last name of the clients and their email address. The second list will include the first and last name of the clients and their mailing addresses, sorted by ZIP code. Additionally, you have been asked to build queries that instantly calculate the total income from all the Winchester Web Design services, and from specific areas such as blogs or shopping carts.

Select Queries

A select query allows you to select records from one or more database tables based on criteria that you set. A select query asks a question, such as, *What are the customer addresses?* or *How much money did the company make last month?* The answer to the question is a set of records. A select query is basically a database inquiry that selects only the records you want to see or edit. The easiest way to create a query is with the Query Wizard.

Query Features

- A query functions like a saved question you ask a database.
- A query produces a subset of data from one or more tables.
- When you edit data in query results, you are actually editing the data stored in the source tables.
- Queries are dynamic objects that display up-to-date data from tables.
- Queries can be used to create forms and reports with fields drawn from multiple tables.

Create→Queries→Query Wizard

DEVELOP YOUR SKILLS: A3-D1

In this exercise, you will use the Query Wizard to create a select query that generates a customer email list.

1. Open **A3-D1-WinWebDesign** from your **Access Chapter 3** folder and save it as `A3-D1-WinWebDesignRevised`.

   When completing exercises, always choose to Enable Content. Notice in the Navigation pane that the database currently has three queries.
2. Choose **Create→Queries→Query Wizard**.

   The Wizard can help you create four types of queries.
3. Click **OK** to accept the Simple Query Wizard.

4. Follow these steps to build the query:

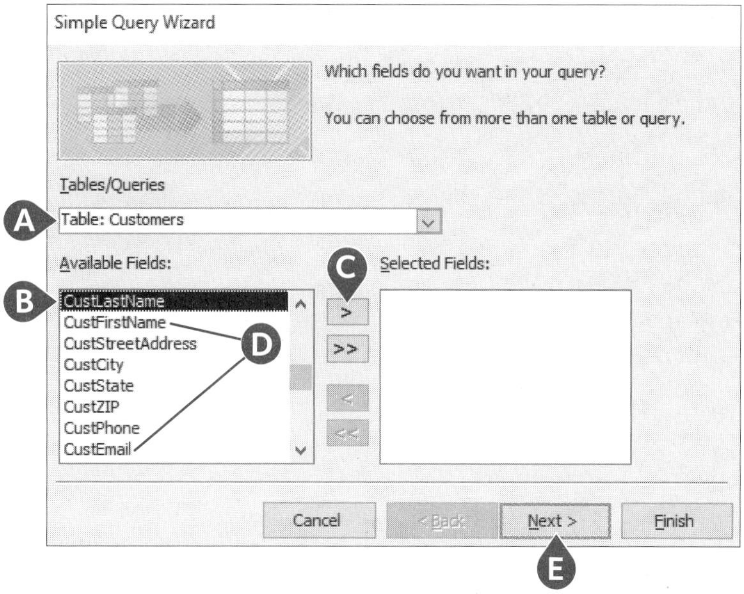

A Make sure the **Customers** table is chosen in the Tables/Queries list. When building a query, you can use multiple tables and even existing queries.

B Choose the **CustLastName** field from the Available Fields list.

C Click the **Add** [>] button to add it to the Selected Fields list.

D Now add the **CustFirstName** and **CustEmail** fields.

E Click **Next**.

If you add the wrong field by accident, double-click the name to move it back to the Available Fields list or select it and use the Move Back [<] *and Move All Back* [<<] *buttons.*

5. Type **`Customers Email List`** as the query title.

6. Make sure the **Open the Query to View Information** option is chosen and click the **Finish** button.

Notice the query results datasheet includes only the three fields you chose from the Customers list.

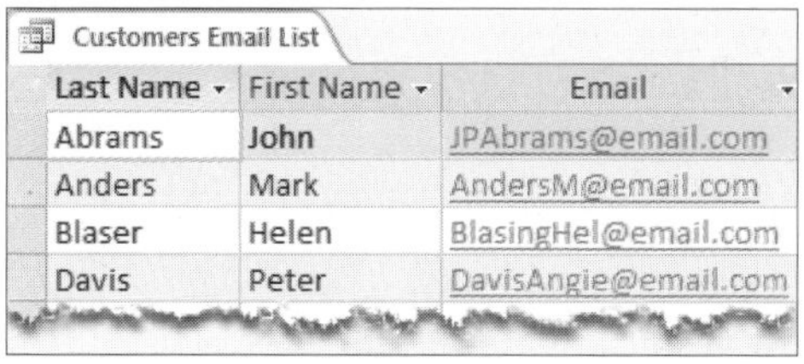

Customers Email List

Last Name	First Name	Email
Abrams	John	JPAbrams@email.com
Anders	Mark	AndersM@email.com
Blaser	Helen	BlasingHel@email.com
Davis	Peter	DavisAngie@email.com

7. Click the **Close** [×] button to the right of the *Customers Email List* tab to close the query.

Creating a Select Query Using Query Design View

Some queries display just a few fields but report on every single record in the table. That may not be a problem for a small table, but when thousands of records and multiple tables are involved, it is often necessary to choose only specific records by setting precise criteria. Using Query Design View, Access allows you to:

- Select fields from multiple tables
- Locate records using criteria from one or more fields
- Perform calculations
- Sort query results and show or hide fields in query results

View the video "Create a Multi-Table Select Query."

Create→Queries→Query Design

DEVELOP YOUR SKILLS: A3-D2

You have already created an email list for the Winchester Web Design customers and now need one for the company's employees. In this exercise, you will create a query to select fields from the Employees table in the Winchester Web Design database and then rearrange the columns in the query grid.

1. Choose **Create→Queries→Query Design** to display the query design grid.

   The Show Table list appears, showing tables and existing queries in the database.

2. Choose the **Employees** table and click the **Add** button.

   The Employees table appears in the design grid.

3. Close the Show Table box and close the Property Sheet box if it is open.

   Next you will add fields from the Employees table to the grid.

4. Double-click the **EmpFirstName** field in the **Employees** table to add it to the grid.

5. Now add the **EmpLastName**, **EmpPhone**, and **EmpEmail** fields to the grid by either double-clicking or dragging them.

Field:	EmpFirstName	EmpLastName	EmpPhone	EmpEmail
Table:	Employees	Employees	Employees	Employees
Sort:				
Show:	☑	☑	☑	☑
Criteria:				
or:				

6. Choose **File→Save** or click the **Save** button on the Quick Access toolbar.

7. Type `Employee Contact Info` as the query name and click **OK**.

8. Click the **Run** ! button.

   Access runs the query and displays four columns of data (First Name, Last Name, Telephone, and Email) for all Employee records.

Rearrange Query Fields

9. Choose **Home→Views→Design View** to switch to Design View.
10. Follow these steps to rearrange the EmpFirstName and EmpLastName fields:

C B A

Field:	EmpFirstName	EmpLastName	EmpPhone	EmpEmail
Table:	Employees	Employees	Employees	Employees
Sort:				
Show:	☑	☑	☑	☑
Criteria:				
or:				

   Ⓐ Click the **EmpLastName** column heading to select the column. The mouse pointer will change to a white arrow, indicating you can now move the column.

   Ⓑ Drag the **EmpLastName** column to the left of the EmpFirstName column until the thick vertical bar is positioned as shown here.

   Ⓒ Release the mouse button to complete the rearrangement.

11. **Run** ! the query.

    Last Name should now appear first in the results.

12. Close the query and save the changes.

Designing a Query Using Multiple Tables

Until now, the datasheets you have worked with have displayed data from only one table. There will be times when you need to view data contained in different tables within the same database. Queries allow you to do this.

Choosing Fields to Include in a Query

When you build a query, you select only those tables and fields that you want to display in the query results datasheet and leave out those fields that have no impact on the data you want to view or that are confidential. By specifying only certain tables and fields in a database and displaying only the desired fields in a query, you can create a report or a form that only presents pertinent data.

Selecting a Field That Appears in Multiple Tables

Multiple tables are only effective in a query if the tables are related. Sometimes the same ID field occurs as a primary key in one table and as a foreign (or secondary) key in another table. If this occurs, always use the table with the primary key in your query.

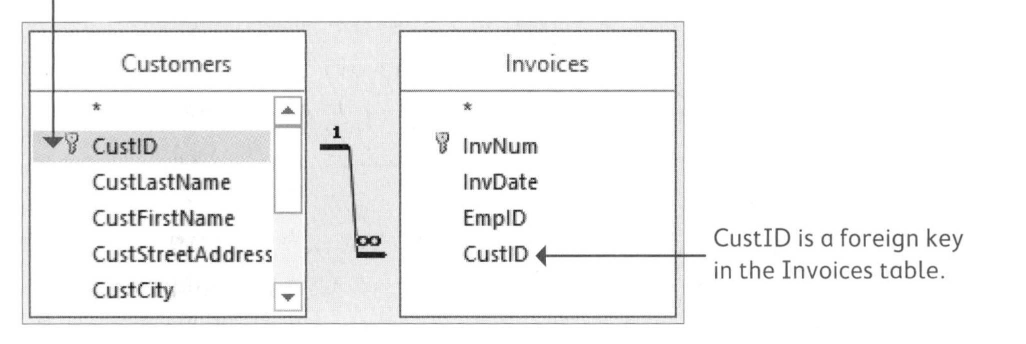

ACCESS

DEVELOP YOUR SKILLS: A3-D3

In this exercise, you will create a multitable query to track the Winchester Web Design invoices by invoice number using Query Design view.

1. Choose **Create→Queries→Query Design** to display the query design grid.
2. Double-click the **Invoices**, **Invoice Details**, and **Products** tables to add them to the query.

   If the Show Table dialog box is not visible, choose Design→Query Setup→Show Table.
3. Close the Show Table box.
4. Double-click the **InvNum**, **InvDate**, and **EmpID** fields in the Invoices table to add those fields to the query grid.
5. Add the **ProdDescription** and **Price** fields from the **Products** table.
6. Add the **Qty** field from the **Invoice Details** table.

   Your query field list should look like this.

Field:	InvNum	InvDate	EmpID	ProdDescription	Price	Qty
Table:	Invoices	Invoices	Invoices	Products	Products	Invoice Details
Sort:						
Show:	☑	☑	☑	☑	☑	☑
Criteria:						
or:						

7. Click the **Sort** box for the InvNum field, click the menu button ▼, and choose **Ascending**.

Field:	InvNum	InvDate
Table:	Invoices	Invoices
Sort:	Ascending	
Show:	☑	☑
Criteria:		
or:		

8. Save the database and save the query as **`InvoicesList`** and click **OK**.
9. Choose **Design→Results→Run** ! to run the query.

   The query results will now be sorted by Invoice Number in the first column.

Using Criteria in Queries

Queries let you specify criteria, which are conditions that field values must meet. Only records meeting the criteria are returned when the query is run.

Field:	InvNum	InvDate	EmpID	ProdDescription	Price	Qty
Table:	Invoices	Invoices	Invoices	Products	Products	Invoice Details
Sort:	Ascending					
Show:	☑	☑	☑	☑	☑	☑
Criteria:			"JFW"			
or:						

In this query, the EmpID criteria is set to JFW.

InvNum	Invoice Date	Emp ID	Description	Price	Qty
1	3 /15/2012	JFW	Secondary Page	$200.00	6
1	3 /15/2012	JFW	Image, Custom Designed	$40.00	11
1	3 /15/2012	JFW	Home Page, Nav, CSS, Design	$400.00	1
5	6 /19/2012	JFW	Image, Custom Designed	$40.00	9

Only records where EmpID is ***JFW*** are returned.

Criteria are commonly used with text, numeric, currency, and date fields. The following table provides a few examples of how criteria are used.

TYPES OF CRITERIA

Field Type	Criteria	Examples of How Records Are Returned
Text	Smith	Last name is Smith
	> =Smith	Last names are from Smith through the end of the alphabet
	Not Smith	Last name is not Smith
Numeric & Currency	> 123	Numeric value is greater than 123
	> =123	Numeric value is greater than or equal to 123
Date	Date( )	Date is today's date
	< Date( ) – 30	The Date field is 30 days or more prior to today's date

Tip! *Search for Query Criteria in Access help for more criteria examples.*

View the video "Create a Query with Criteria."

DEVELOP YOUR SKILLS: A3-D4

In this exercise, you will add criteria to the query grid and run the query.

1. If necessary, open the **InvoicesList** query and switch to **Design View**.
2. Click the **Criteria** box for the EmpID field, type **`JFW`**, and tap Enter.

   Access will apply quotation marks indicating this is a literal value.

Field:	InvNum	InvDate	EmpID
Table:	Invoices	Invoices	Invoices
Sort:	Ascending		
Show:	☑	☑	☑
Criteria:			"JFW"
or:			

3. Choose **Design→Results→Run** to run the query.

   The query results now only include records where the EmpID is equal to JFW.

4. Close the query and choose **No** when prompted to save the changes.

   Saving changes to the query at this time would save the JFW criteria as part of the query. However, you will continue to use the query for all employees.

ACCESS

Wildcard Characters

Wildcard characters are used to locate records that have similar but not identical data. They help you locate records that match a pattern. For example, you might want to find all customers with last names that begin with the letter *B* or all products that begin with the word *Blog*.

WILDCARD CHARACTERS

Common Wildcard Symbols	How They Are Used
Asterisk (*)	Substitutes for a group of characters that appear at the position of the asterisk **Example**: *R** in the last name field will locate all last names beginning with *R* regardless of how many characters make up the name. In this case, *Rogers, Rich,* and *Rodriquez* would all appear in the results datasheet.
Question mark (?)	Substitutes for a single character that might appear at the position of the question mark **Example**: *m?s* will locate records containing values such as *mrs, ms,* and *mbs.*
Open/close brackets [ ]	Matches text or individual characters placed within the brackets individually **Example**: *ca[rt]* will find *cat* and *car* but not *cab* or *cad.*

Tip! *Search for Wildcard Characters in Access help for more wildcard symbols and examples.*

AND and OR Criteria

In some cases, you may need to locate records that meet multiple criteria. This can be done using AND and OR conditions. For example, you may want to locate all records where the employee is web certified AND lives in Sarasota. Or you may want to locate all employees who live in Sarasota OR Bradenton.

Field:	CustID	CustFirstName	CustLastName	CustCity
Table:	Customers	Customers	Customers	Customers
Sort:				
Show:	☑	☑	☑	☑
Criteria:				"Sarasota"
or:				"Bradenton"

Create an OR condition by adding a second criterion to the Or row of a field.

Field:	InvNum	InvDate	ProdDescription	Price	Qty
Table:	Invoices	Invoices	Products	Products	Invoice Details
Sort:	Ascending				
Show:	☑	☑	☑	☑	☑
Criteria:			"Image"		>10

Create an AND condition by adding another criterion to a different field on the Criteria row.

DEVELOP YOUR SKILLS: A3-D5

In this exercise, you will use wildcards to locate variable data and set multiple criteria in a query to find out which customers have gotten blogs and which customers have added more than ten images at a time to their websites.

1. Open the **Invoices Query** query in **Design View**.
2. Follow these steps to use wildcard characters and to use AND and OR criteria:

Field:	InvNum	InvDate	ProdDescription	Price	Qty	LineTotal: [Qty]*[Price]
Table:	Invoices	Invoices	Products	Products	Invoice Details	
Sort:						
Show:	☑	☑	☑	☑	☑	☑
Criteria:			Like "Blog*"			
or:			Like "Image*"		>10	

A. Click in the **ProdDescription Criteria** box, type **`Blog*`**, and tap Enter.

   Access converts Blog* *to* Like "Blog*".

B. Click in the ProdDescription **Or** box, type **`Image*`**, and tap Enter.

C. Click in the Qty **Or** box and type **> 10**. Be sure to type in the same row as *Like "Image*"* (the *Or* row).

   These criteria will choose records where ProdDescription begins with Blog *OR ProdDescription begins with* Image *AND the Qty is greater than 10.*

3. **Run** ! the query.

   Access displays the records that meet the specified criteria: either a blog or a transaction with more than ten images.

4. Close the query and save the changes.

Date Criteria

You can set date criteria to determine age, hired date, invoice date, and so forth. Access acknowledges the same comparison criteria for performing date comparisons that it does for locating other types of data, regardless of the format used to enter dates.

DATE CRITERIA

Criterion	Examples of How Records Are Returned
06/22/2013	Date is 06/22/2013
<22-Oct-2013	Dates that occur before 22/Oct/2013
>01/01/13	Dates that occur after 01/01/13
Between 01/01/13 and 06/30/13	Dates between 01/01/2013 and 06/30/2013

DEVELOP YOUR SKILLS: A3-D6

Winchester Web Design needs to track all invoices issued in 2012. In this exercise, you will query the database to locate customers with invoices dated from January 1, 2012, through December 31, 2012.

1. Choose **Create→Queries→Query Design**.
2. Use double clicks to add the **Customers**, **Invoices**, **Invoice Details**, and **Products** tables to the query.
3. Close the Show Table box.
4. Double-click **InvNum** and **InvDate** in the **Invoices** table to add those fields to the query grid.
5. Add the **CustID** field from the **Customers** table.
6. Add the **Qty** field from the **Invoice Details** table.
7. Add the **ProdDescription** and **Price** fields from the **Products** table.
8. Widen the InvDate field by dragging the column heading to the right as shown here.

   You will enter a long entry in the next step, and widening the InvDate column will allow you to see the entire entry.

InvDate	CustID
Invoices	Customers
☑	☑

9. Click in the **Criteria** box for the InvDate field, type `Between January 1, 2012 and December 31, 2012`, and then tap Enter.

   Access will format the expression, and your query grid should now match the following example. Regardless of how you type the dates, whether January 1, 2012; 01/01/12; or 1-1-2012, Access formats the date after you enter it so that it appears as #1/1/2012#.

Field:	InvNum	InvDate	CustID	Qty	ProdDescription	Price
Table:	Invoices	Invoices	Customers	Invoice Details	Products	Products
Sort:						
Show:	☑	☑	☑	☑	☑	☑
Criteria:		Between #1/1/2012# And #12/31/2012#				
or:						

10. **Run** ! the query.

    Notice that only records with a date in 2012 appear in the results.

11. Choose **File→Save** or click the **Save** button on the Quick Access toolbar.
12. Save the query as `Invoices2012` and then close it.

Sorting, Showing, and Limiting Results

The query grid contains a Sort row that lets you sort the query results. At times you may also want to use fields to specify criteria but may not want those fields to be displayed in the query results. This can be accomplished by unchecking the Show box for the desired field(s).

Limiting the Number of Results Displayed

Large databases with millions of records often return so many records that it can be challenging to find what you are looking for. So limiting the number of records displayed can be beneficial, especially when these records are sorted.

For example, if you set up a query to sort in descending order and then limit the number of items displayed to ten, you would, in effect, have a list of the top ten items in the table being queried. The Return feature lets you set the number of records to be displayed, or returned, in the query results.

Design→Query Setup→Return

DEVELOP YOUR SKILLS: A3-D7

In this exercise, you will create a query that sets a sort order and you will hide a field from displaying in the query results. You will also limit the number of records returned.

1. Choose **Create→Queries→Query Design** .
2. Use double clicks to add the **Customers**, **Invoices**, **Invoice Details**, and **Products** tables to the query.
3. Close the Show Table box.
4. Double-click the **CustID**, **CustFirstName**, and **CustLastName** fields in the **Customers** table to add them to the design grid.
5. Add the **InvDate** field from the **Invoices** table.
6. Add the **ProdDescription** field from the **Products** table.
7. Add the **Qty** field from the **Invoice Details** table.
8. Follow these steps to set a criterion and set the sort order:

Field:	CustID	CustFirstName	CustLastName	InvDate	ProdDescription	Qty
Table:	Customers	Customers	Customers	Invoices	Products	Invoice Detai
Sort:						Descending
Show:	☑	☑	☑	☑	☑	☑
Criteria:					Like "Image"	
or:						

A Click in the **ProdDescription** criteria box, type **Image***, and tap Enter. Access converts *Image** to *Like "Image*"*. This criterion will choose only records where the product description begins with *Image*.

B Click in the **Sort** box for the Qty field and choose **Descending** from the list of sort options.

ACCESS

9. **Run** ! the query.

   Notice the records are sorted in descending order (largest to smallest) by quantity.

   CustID is an important key to have in the query because it is a primary key field. But it isn't needed in the query results because it contains the same information that appears in the CustFirstName and CustLastName fields. So you will hide it from the query results.

10. Choose **Home→Views→Design View** to switch back to Design View.
11. Uncheck the **Show** box for the **CustID** field and **Run** ! the query.

    The CustID field is still part of the query design, but it no longer shows in the query results.

12. Switch back to **Design View** and choose **Design→Query Setup→Return** **menu button ▼**.
13. Choose **5** from the list and run the query.

    The query returns seven records (not five). This is because the query returns all records with the five largest quantities. But three records had a Qty of 14, which is the fifth highest amount, so all of those records were returned, increasing the total to seven records.

14. Save the query as `Most Images` and then close it.

Calculated Fields

Calculated fields are formulas that perform calculations on other query fields. Calculated fields are added to queries and are not part of the underlying query tables. They are added to the query design grid and their calculated results then appear in the query results. A calculated field:

- Creates a new field in a query that can also be used in a form or report
- Can be used to perform mathematical operations such as addition and multiplication
- Has a name and can be formatted with properties just like a regular field
- Enables you to combine values in two text fields into one field such as LastName and FirstInitial
- Updates and recalculates each time you run the query

Identifying Parts of a Calculated Field

The structure of a calculated field includes a field name and a mathematical expression. Two examples of calculated fields in an Access query would be Wage: Hours * Rate and Total: Price * Quantity, where Wage and Price are calculated field names and Hours * Rate and Price * Quantity are the calculations that are performed.

Price	Qty	LineTotal: [Price]*[Qty]
Products	Invoice Details	
☑	☑	☑

The LineTotal calculated field multiplies Price * Qty

Price	Qty	LineTotal
$200.00	6	$1,200.00
$40.00	11	$440.00
$400.00	1	$400.00
$40.00	15	$600.00

The query results

Each calculated field can contain the following elements.

CALCULATED FIELD ELEMENTS

Element	Description
Calculated field name	This is the unique name you assign to the field and is followed by a colon (:) to separate the field name from the expression.
Field names from existing tables	Field names from the query can be added to the calculated field expression. Access adds brackets [ ] around field names.
Arithmetic or comparison operators	Use +, –, *, /, ( ), ^, <, =, > to perform mathematical operations or compare values.
Concatenation (i.e., linking together)	An ampersand (&) can be used to join text values from multiple fields. For example, FirstName&LastName. Spaces can be added between fields by using quotation marks around a single space (" "). For example, the quotation marks in FirstName& " " &LastName create a space between the first and last names in the query results.

Calculated Field Properties

You can set field properties such as size, number format, and default values within tables. Likewise, you can set field properties in calculated fields. This is almost always needed in calculated fields as the query results need to be formatted with the correct number of decimal places, commas, currency format, and other formatting as needed. Field properties are set using the field Property Sheet.

Design→Show/Hide→Property Sheet

DEVELOP YOUR SKILLS: A3-D8

In this exercise, you will create and format a calculated field.

1. Open the **InvoicesList** query and switch to **Design View**.
2. Click in the **first cell** of the blank column next to the *Qty* field.

Price	Qty	
Products	Invoice Details	
☑	☑	☐
	>10	

3. Type the calculated field expression **`LineTotal:Price * Qty`**, making sure you include the colon between *LineTotal* and *Price*.
4. Tap Enter.

   Access will format your expression by adding brackets to field names.

   The name of your calculated field is LineTotal, *and it will multiply the Price times the Qty in each record when the query is run. Your completed field should match the following.*

Field:	InvNum	InvDate	EmpID	ProdDescription	Price	Qty	LineTotal: [Price]*[Qty]
Table:	Invoices	Invoices	Invoices	Products	Products	Invoice Details	
Sort:	Ascending						
Show:	☑	☑	☑	☑	☑	☑	☑
Criteria:							
or:							

5. Right-click anywhere in your calculated field column and choose **Properties**.
6. Set the Format property to **Currency** and type `Line Total` in the **Caption** field.

   The currency format will display the calculated results with a dollar sign and two decimals. The caption will become the column heading for your calculated field in the query results.
7. **Run** [!] the query, and your calculated field results will appear as shown below.

Invoices List

InvNum	Invoice Date	Emp ID	Description	Price	Qty	Line Total
1	3/15/2012	JFW	Secondary Page	$200.00	6	$1,200.00
1	3/15/2012	JFW	Image, Custom Designed	$40.00	11	$440.00
1	3/15/2012	JFW	Home Page, Nav, CSS, Design	$400.00	1	$400.00
2	4/2/2012	MJW	Image, Custom Designed	$40.00	15	$600.00
2	4/2/2012	MJW	Home Page, Nav, CSS, Design	$400.00	1	$400.00
2	4/2/2012	MJW	Secondary Page	$200.00	7	$1,400.00

8. Save and close the query and then close the A3-D1-WinWebDesignRevised database.

Self-Assessment

Check your knowledge of this chapter's key concepts and skills using the Self-Assessment in your ebook or eLab course.

Reinforce Your Skills

REINFORCE YOUR SKILLS: A3-R1

Create Queries Using Criteria and Wildcards

Kids for Change is planning to fine-tune their database by adding queries that enable them to track activities as well as staff/volunteer availability. In this exercise, you will create various queries that will yield the desired information.

1. Open the **A3-R1-K4C** database from your **Access Chapter 3** folder and save it as `A3-R1-K4CRevised`.

Create a Query Using the Query Wizard

2. Choose **Create→Queries→Query Wizard**.
3. Choose **Simple Query Wizard** and click **OK**.
4. Choose the **Activities** table and add the **Activity**, **Location**, **Day**, and **MeetTime** fields to the **Selected Fields** list.
5. Click **Next**, name the query `Activities List`, and finish the query.
6. Review the query results and then close the query.

Create a Query in Design View

7. Choose **Create→Queries→Query Design** to start a new query.
8. Add the **Volunteers** table and then close the Show Table box.
9. Use double clicks or drag and drop to add the **VolLastName**, **VolFirstName**, **VolPhone**, and **VolDay** fields to the query design grid (in that order).
10. Run the query and take a moment to review the results.

    Now you will change the field order.
11. Switch to **Design View**.
12. Click the **VolDay** field heading to select the field.
13. Drag the **VolDay** field, dropping it in front of the *VolLastName* field.

Field:	VolDay	VolLastName	VolFirstName	VolPhone
Table:	Volunteers	Volunteers	Volunteers	Volunteers
Sort:				
Show:	☑	☑	☑	☑
Criteria:				
or:				

14. **Run** the query and review the results.
15. Save the query as `Volunteer List` and then close it.

Create a Multi-Table Query

16. Create a new query in **Query Design** view and add the **Activities** and **Staff** tables to the query.
17. Add the **Activity**, **Day**, and **MeetTime** fields from the **Activities** table to the query design grid.
18. Add the **StaffLastName**, **StaffFirstName**, and **StaffPhone** fields from the **Staff** table.
19. Set the **Sort** option for the Activity field to **Ascending**.

ACCESS

20. **Run** ! the query and view the results.

21. Save the query as **`Activity Staffing List`** and then close it.

Add Wildcard and AND/OR Criteria to a Query

22. Right-click the **Activity Staffing List** query in the Navigation pane and choose **Design View**.

    You can open a query in Design View using this method or you can run it first and then switch to Design View. Remember to try right-clicks if you are having trouble finding commands.

23. Create a Saturday or Sunday OR condition in the Day field as shown here.

    Typing the quotation marks " " isn't necessary, as Access will add them for you.

Field:	Activity	Day	MeetTime
Table:	Activities	Activities	Activities
Sort:	Ascending		
Show:	☑	☑	☑
Criteria:		"Saturday"	
or:		"Sunday"	

24. Run the query.

    Only activities for Saturday or Sunday should be displayed.

25. Switch to **Design View**.

26. Remove the "Sunday" OR condition by deleting it.

27. Now enter **`12:00`** in the MeetTime **Criteria** field as shown here, tapping Enter when finished.

    This creates a Saturday AND 12:00 meet-time condition. Access will format the 12:00 condition like this: #12:00:00 PM#.

Field:	Activity	Day	MeetTime
Table:	Activities	Activities	Activities
Sort:	Ascending		
Show:	☑	☑	☑
Criteria:		"Saturday"	#12:00:00 PM#
or:			

28. Run the query.

    Just one activity meeting, the AND condition (a car wash), should be returned by the query.

29. Switch to **Design View** and remove both the *Saturday* and *12:00* criteria.

30. Type **`S*`** in the **Criteria** box for the Day field and tap Enter.

    *Access recognizes the asterisk * wildcard character and formats the condition as* Like "S*"*. This should return all records where the name of the day begins with S (Saturday and Sunday). This should produce the same results as when you used the Saturday OR Sunday condition earlier in this exercise.*

31. Run the query and take a moment to observe the results.

32. Save the changes and close the query.

Add Date Criteria to a New Query

Now you will create a query that returns the records of the youngest children so you can determine which children may need more supervision.

33. Create a new query in **Design View** and add only the **Children** table to the query.

34. Add the **ChildLastName**, **ChildFirstName**, and **BirthDate** fields to the query.

35. Run the query and take a moment to observe the results.

    Now you will add a condition.

36. Switch to **Design View**, type **>January 1, 2005** in the BirthDate **Criteria** field, and tap [Enter] when finished.

    Once again Access will apply formatting to the criterion.

37. Run the query.

    Only records where the child was born after January 1, 2005, should be displayed.

38. Choose **File→Save** or click the **Save** button on the Quick Access toolbar and save the query with the name **Younger Children**.

39. Close the query and then close the **A3-R1-K4CRevised** database.

REINFORCE YOUR SKILLS: A3-R2

Limit the Records Returned and Use Calculated Fields

Kids for Change is planning to fine-tune their database by adding queries that will produce calculated results. You are in charge of their IT department, and it is your responsibility to generate the desired query results.

1. Open the **A3-R2-K4C** database from your **Access Chapter 3** folder and save it as **A3-R2-K4CRevised**.

Limit and Sort Query Results

2. Run the **Children List** query.

    The query returns the records of all children in the database in alphabetical order by last name.

3. Switch to **Design View** and choose **Design→Query Setup→Return menu button ▼**.
4. Choose **5** from the list.
5. Click in the **Sort** box for the BirthDate field and choose **Descending**.
6. Run the query.

    Only the records for the five youngest children should be displayed.

7. Close the query, saving the changes.

Add a Calculated Field and Format the Field

As part of their community give-back policy, Kids for Change puts 10 percent of all donations into a scholarship fund. Now you will add a field that calculates 10 percent of each donation.

8. Run the **Donations Query** query and take a moment to observe the results.
9. Switch to **Design View** and scroll to the right in the query grid until the first empty column is visible.

    You will enter a calculated field in this column.

10. Type **ScholarFund:Amount*.1** in the first cell (the Field cell) of the empty column, being sure to include the colon between *ScholarFund* and *Amount*.
11. Tap [Enter] to complete the calculated field, and if necessary, widen the column so you can see the entire calculated field.

12. Right-click anywhere in your calculated field column and choose **Properties** to display the Property Sheet for the field.
13. Click in the **Format** box and choose **Currency** from the drop-down list.
14. Type `Scholar Fund` in the **Caption** box.
15. Run the query and take a moment to ensure that the calculated field is calculating correctly and is formatted with the Currency format.
16. Close the query, saving the changes.
17. Close the database.

REINFORCE YOUR SKILLS: A3-R3

Create Select Queries Using Criteria and Calculated Fields

Kids for Change is planning to fine-tune their database by adding queries that will produce calculated and formatted results based on specific search criteria.

1. Open the **A3-R3-K4C** database from your **Access Chapter 3** folder and save it as `A3-R3-K4CRevised`.

Create a Query Using the Query Wizard

2. Use the **Query Wizard** to create a simple query and choose the **Donors** table.
3. Add the **DonorLName**, **DonorFName**, **DonorPhone**, and **DonorEmail** fields to the query.
4. Use `Donor Contact List` as the query name and finish the query.
5. Review the query results and close the query.

Create a Query in Design View

6. Create a new query using **Query Design** view and add the **Staff** table to the query.
7. Add the **StaffLastName, StaffFirstName**, **StaffStreet**, **StaffCity**, **StaffST**, and **StaffZIP** fields.
8. Save the query as `Staff Mailing List`, **Run** the query, and review the results.
9. Close the query.

Create a Multi-Table Query

10. Create a new query using **Query Design** view and add the **Activities** and **Children** tables to the design grid.
11. Add the **Activity**, **Day**, and **MeetTime** fields from the **Activities** table.
12. Add the **ChildLastName**, **ChildFirstName**, and **ChildPhone** fields from the **Children** table.
13. Save the query as `Participant List`.
14. Run the query and review the results.

Add Criteria

Now you will add criteria to the Participant List query to list the children signed up for 9:00 AM Saturday activities.

15. Switch to **Design View**.

16. Create an AND condition by setting **Saturday** as a criterion in the Day field and **9:00** as a criterion in the MeetTime field.
17. Run the query.

    Notice the only records returned are those where the day is Saturday AND the meet time is 9:00.
18. Close the query, saving the changes.

Use Wildcard Criteria

Now you will use a wildcard to select nearby donors so they can be invited to local activities.

19. Right-click the **Donations Query** query in the Navigation pane and choose **Design View**.
20. If necessary, scroll right through the field list until you locate the DonorZIP field.
21. Enter **34*** in the DonorZIP **Criteria** field.

    The asterisk is a wildcard character.
22. Run the query.

    Only records where the ZIP code begins with 34 are returned by the query.

Add Date Criteria

23. Switch to **Design View** and remove the **Criteria** from the DonorZIP field.
24. Enter **>01/01/2013** in the DonationDate **Criteria** field.
25. Run the query and review the results.

Sort and Limit Query Results

26. Switch to **Design View**.
27. Set the **DonationDate** field to sort in **Descending** order.
28. Use the **Design→Query Setup→Return** **menu button ▼** list to limit the records returned to **5**.
29. Run the query and review the results.

Add a Calculated Field and Format the Field

30. Switch to **Design View**.
31. Set the Return number back to **All**.
32. Create a calculated field by entering **NetAmt:Amount-ScholarFund** in the first empty column's **Field** row.
33. Right-click anywhere in the new calculated field column and open the Property Sheet.
34. Set the Format to **Currency** and type **Net Donation** as the **Caption**.
35. Run the query and review the results.
36. Close the query, saving the changes.
37. Close the database.

ACCESS

Apply Your Skills

APPLY YOUR SKILLS: A3-A1

Create Queries Using Criteria and Wildcards

The new CEO of Universal Corporate Events, has asked you to refine a number of queries to be more selective in data output. In this exercise, you will create queries; add criteria, wildcards, and AND/OR conditions to a query; and add date criteria to a query.

1. Open the **A3-A1-UCE** database from your **Access Chapter 3** folder and save it as **`A3-A1-UCERevised`**.

Create a Query Using the Query Wizard

2. Use the **Query Wizard** to create a simple select query and choose the **Personnel** table.
3. Add the **PerLastName**, **PerFirstName**, **PerPhone**, and **PerEmail** fields.
4. Use the query name **`Personnel Contact List`** and finish the query.
5. Review the results and then close the query.

Create a Multi-Table Query in Design View

6. Create a query in **Design View** that uses the **Events**, **Schedules**, and **Menus** tables.
7. Add the following fields to the query:

   Events Table: **EventName**

   Schedules Table: **VenueID**, **ContactID**, **EventDate**, **Guests**

   Menus Table: **MenuPlan**, **Chg/PP**
8. Run the query and review the results.
9. Save the query as **`Event List`** then close it.

Use Wildcards and AND/OR Criteria

UCE, Ltd. is planning a recruiting event in Sarasota and would like to contact employees from greater Sarasota (area code 941) to involve them in planning the event. You will modify a query to return the records of personnel who live in the Sarasota area.

10. Open the **Personnel Contact List** query in **Design View**.
11. Type the wildcard text **`*941*`** in the PerPhone **Criteria** field.
12. Run the query and verify that each telephone number in the query results contains *941* somewhere in the number.
13. Close the query, saving the changes.
14. Create a new query in **Design View** from the **Venues** table that includes the **VenueName**, **VenueCity**, **VenuePhone**, and **VenueWebSite** fields.
15. Type **`Sarasota`** in the VenueCity **Criteria** field and **`Tampa`** in the **Or** row of the **VenueCity** field.
16. Run the query and verify that the city is *Sarasota* or *Tampa* in each record.
17. Save the query as **`Tampa-Sarasota Venues`** and then close the query.

Add Date Criteria

18. Run the **Event List** query and notice the range of dates.
19. Switch to **Design View** and type `>May 1, 2014` in the EventDate **Criteria** field.
20. Sort the query in **Ascending** order on the **EventDate** field.
21. Run the query and make sure it produces the intended results.
22. Close the query, saving the changes, and then close the database.

APPLY YOUR SKILLS: A3-A2

Limit the Records Returned and Use Calculated Fields

You've been asked to improve UCE data retrieval and formatting. In this exercise, you will sort and limit records returned in query results and create a query using a calculated field.

1. Open the **A3-A2-UCE** database from your **Access Chapter 3** folder and save it as `A3-A2-UCERevised`.

Limit and Sort Query Results

2. Run the **Event Revenue** query and review the results.
3. Switch to **Design View** and set the sort order of the **TotalRev** calculated field to **Descending**.
4. Set the Return number to **5** to limit the number of records returned by the query to the top five.
5. Run the query and review the results.
6. Switch to **Design View** and change the Return value back to **All**.

Add a Calculated Field and Format the Field

7. Use the name and expression `Comm:TotalRev*.08` to create a calculated field.
8. Open the Property Sheet for the new calculated field and set the Format to **Currency** and use `Commission` as the Caption.
9. Run the query and review the results.
10. Close the query, saving the changes, and then close the database.

APPLY YOUR SKILLS: A3-A3

Create Select Queries Using Criteria and Calculated Fields

In this exercise, you will create and modify a number of queries for more precise, targeted data selection for Universal Corporate Events.

1. Open the **A3-A3-UCE** database from your **Access Chapter 3** folder and save it as `A3-A3-UCERevised`.

Add a Wildcard Criterion

To begin, you will create a query to list contact information for the event venues that have an 800 telephone number so they can be reached by phone at no charge to the caller.

2. Create a simple query that uses the **Venues** table to generate a list of venue names and their corresponding phone numbers and websites.

3. Name the query `TollFreeVenues`.
4. In **Design View**, add the wildcard text `*800*` to the **Criteria** row to return only records where the Venue Phone number has *800* in it.
5. Run the query and resize the columns in the query results so that all the data is visible.
6. Close the query, saving the changes.

Add Wildcard and Date Criteria and Sort the Query

Because June is the most popular month for weddings, UCE wants to pay special attention to weddings scheduled for June so they can hire extra part-time workers.

7. Use the **Query Wizard** to create a new simple query that uses the **Event List** query as a record source.
8. Include all of the Events List query fields in the new query.
9. Leave the Wizard's Detail or Summary option set to **Detail**.
10. Name the query `June Weddings` and finish the query.
11. Switch to **Design View**.
12. Add the wildcard text `Wed*` (for *Weddings*) to the EventName **Criteria** field.
13. Set the sort order of the EventDate field to **Ascending**.
14. Enter the text `Between June 1, 2014 and June 30, 2014` in the EventDate **Criteria** field.
15. Run the query and review the results.
16. Close the query, saving the changes.

Limit the Number of Records in Query Results

Now you will sort the Location Scheduling query by the largest number of guests, and return the ten highest values so the company can focus extra personnel and resources to those events if the guests are scheduled for a full menu plan.

17. Display the **Location Scheduling** query in **Design View**.
18. Sort the query in **Descending** order by **Guests**.
19. Set the number of records returned to `10`.

    You'll need to click in the Return box and type 10. If Access changes the 10 to 100, delete the extra zero (0).
20. Run the query and review the results.
21. Close the query, saving the changes.

Add and Format Calculated Fields

Now you will add a calculated field that subtracts the venue contact's commission from the total revenue to result in a net revenue amount.

22. Display the **Event Revenue** query in **Design View**.
23. Add a calculated field named `NetRev` that subtracts **Comm** from **TotalRev**.
24. Format the new field as **Currency**, and give it the Caption `Net Revenue`.

25. Add a criterion to the **TotalRev** field to only choose records where the TotalRev is greater than 3000.
26. Run the query and review the results.
27. Close the query, saving the changes, and then close the database.

Extend Your Skills

These exercises challenge you to think critically and apply your new skills. You will be evaluated on your ability to follow directions, completeness, creativity, and the use of proper grammar and mechanics. Save files to your chapter folder. Submit assignments as directed.

A3-E1 That's the Way I See It

Blue Jean Landscaping needs queries to better manage its customer and equipment lists. Open the **A3-E1-BJL** database and save it as **A3-E1-BJLRevised**. Create a query named **813 Area Code** that uses all fields from the Customers table. The query should return only customers with a phone area code of *813* sorted in ascending order by city. Create another query named **Equipment Value** that uses all fields from the Equipment table. Use a calculated field named **EquipValue** to determine the total value of equipment by multiplying the Cost by the quantity In Stock. Sort the results with the largest Equipment Values appearing first and format the EquipValue field using the Currency format.

A3-E2 Be Your Own Boss

Blue Jean Landscaping wants to devise more targeted data retrieval. Open the **A3-E2-BJL** database and save it as **A3-E2-BJLRevised**. Create a query that will return a contact list for BJL's customers sorted by last name. Create another query that creates a customer mailing list sorted by ZIP code. Use a wildcard to select only records where the zip code begins with **33**. Add a calculated field to the Sales Invoices query that multiplies Cost by Qty Sold to produce a total. Format the new field as Currency and assign it a caption. Finally, limit the number of records returned to the largest five invoice totals, so those customers can be targeted for preferred customer offers.

A3-E3 Demonstrate Proficiency

You've been asked by the management at Stormy BBQ to query their database. Open the **A3-E3-StormyBBQ** database and save it as **A3-E3-StormyBBQRevised**. Create a query that uses data from the DailyReceipts table and determines the total revenue received for each item using the ItemPrice and QtySold fields. Include all fields from the table in the query and sort in descending order on the field that is used to perform the daily total calculations. Create another query using the Merchandise table that contains all fields from the Merchandise table and a sequence of calculated fields. For each item, the calculated fields should determine the Stock Cost of that item (Cost * Stock), the List Price Revenue if all items were sold at list price (Listprice * Stock), and the Profit, which is the difference between the revenue and cost.

ACCESS

4 Using Reports to Display Information

In this chapter, you will create reports to organize and summarize data into meaningful information. Although reports can summarize data from a single database table, they often present specific data from multiple tables or from queries based on multiple tables. Both forms and reports use many of the same tools and techniques to organize and present information in a readable format.

LEARNING OBJECTIVES

- Create basic reports using the Report tool
- Create reports with the Report Wizard
- Change field alignment and size in Layout View
- Change field properties
- Insert logos and dates
- Insert new fields

Project: Turning Data into Information with Reports

Forms are great for entering data and displaying single records. Most businesses, however, want to filter and summarize data, as well as display specific data, such as running totals, in a readable format. Winchester Web Design needs a new report to summarize the sales for each employee and display sales totals. As its database manager, you have agreed to create a report to meet these needs.

Introducing Reports

Because reports are often presented in a readable format and end up as a printout, there are some basics that every report should include. Of course it should be well organized, look professional, and be visually appealing. Imagine finding a report on your desk without a date, without page numbers, or without a title that states what it is for. How might this affect the usability and readability of the data?

Most reports should have both a title and a subtitle. The title may simply be the company name. The subtitle should state specifically what the report is for, such as Monthly Income or Product List. Every report requires a date and should include the page number, even if the report is only one page. Once you have a good handle on the who, what, and when, you will be ready to create your first report.

Basic Reports

Use the Report button to instantly create a basic report for a selected table or query. This is the easiest way to create a report using all of the fields from the table or query. Only one table or query can be used in a basic report.

Create→Reports→Report

DEVELOP YOUR SKILLS: A4-D1

In this exercise, you will create a basic report.

1. Open **A4-D1-WinWebDesign** from your **Access Chapter 4** folder and save it as **A4-D1-WinWebDesignRevised**.

   Click the Enable Content button, should it appear.

2. Choose the **Products** table in the Navigation pane.
3. Choose **Create→Reports→Report**.

   A basic report is displayed in Layout View. In Layout View you can easily move and size report objects.

4. Close any boxes that may be open, such as the Property Sheet or field list pane.
5. Choose **Home→View→Report View**.

   Report View is best for presenting reports.

6. Choose **Home→View→Print Preview** to see how your report will look when printed.

   Any problems the report might have can be corrected using Layout and Design Views.

7. Click the **Close Print Preview** button on the right side of the Ribbon.

8. Switch to **Design View**.

   The report body contains sections that are populated with text labels and controls that display the date, time, and other data and perform calculations.

9. Take a moment to mouse over the design tools and review the ToolTips that appear.
10. Choose **File→Save** or click the **Save** button on the Quick Access toolbar and save the report as **`Products`**.
11. Close the report.

Report Organization and Structure

Reports can display data from multiple tables and even from queries. Report data must often be grouped and sorted so it can be easily analyzed and interpreted. Effective reports turn data into information by displaying it in an organized and understandable manner. Queries are often the best data source for reports as they can receive data from multiple tables, sort the data, and even include calculated fields.

Sections

Sections provide the structure needed to effectively organize and present information. There are several types of sections, with each type used for a specific purpose.

REPORT SECTIONS

Section(s)	Description
Report Header and Footer	Displayed only at the top of the first page and bottom of the last page. Some uses include titles, subtitles, and logos.
Page Header and Footer	Displayed at the top and bottom of every page. Some uses include descriptive labels, page numbers, and dates.
Group Header and Footer	The group header shows the fields on which report data is grouped. For example, grouping by Sales Person might list each sales person and all the transactions that person is responsible for. The group footer displays summary information such as the total of all transactions for each sales person.
Detail	Main part of the report where the records are displayed. The records are typically organized in groups. The detail sections are where field headings appear.

The following image shows a report in Layout View with the various sections highlighted.

Winchester Web Design

Invoices for Q1 2013

Winchester WEB DESIGN

The Report Header appears at the top of the report.

ACCESS

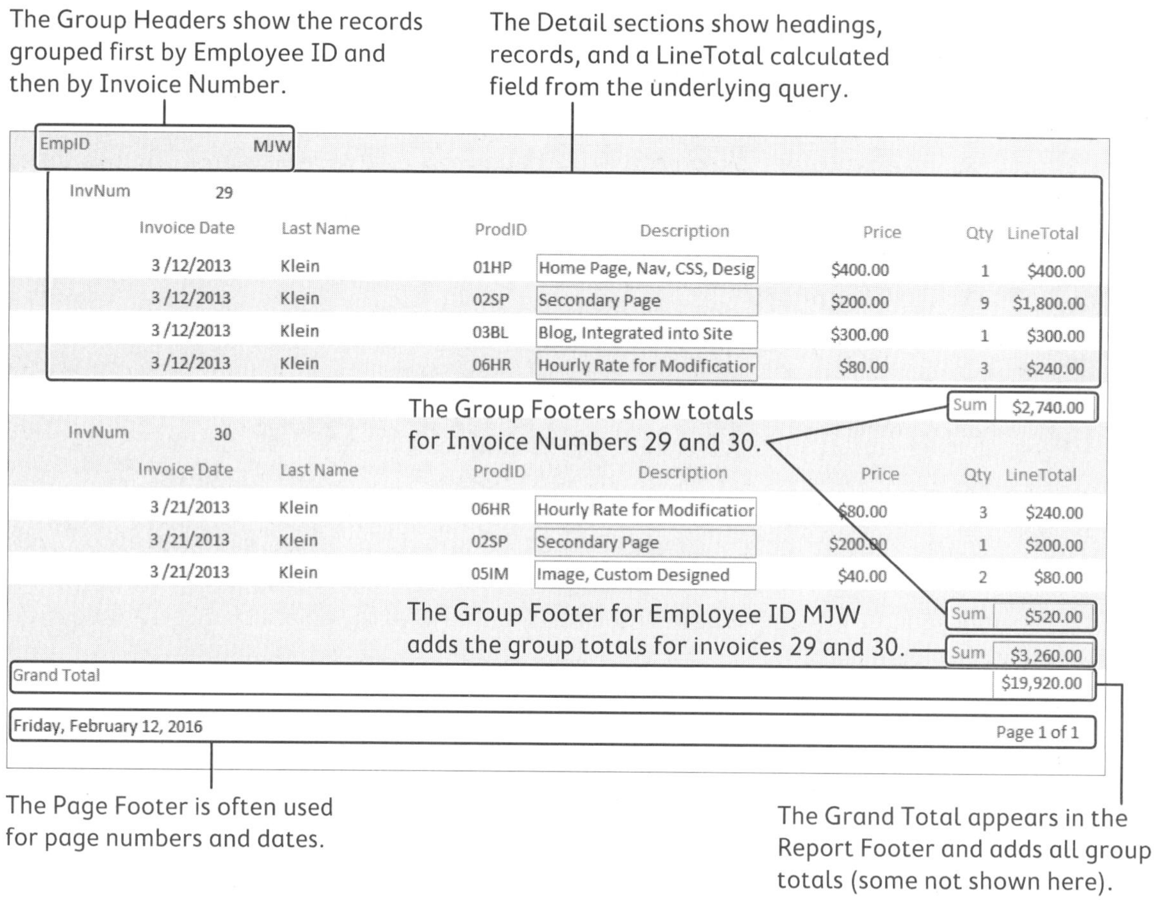

The Group Headers show the records grouped first by Employee ID and then by Invoice Number.

The Detail sections show headings, records, and a LineTotal calculated field from the underlying query.

EmpID MJW

InvNum 29

Invoice Date	Last Name	ProdID	Description	Price	Qty	LineTotal
3 /12/2013	Klein	01HP	Home Page, Nav, CSS, Desig	$400.00	1	$400.00
3 /12/2013	Klein	02SP	Secondary Page	$200.00	9	$1,800.00
3 /12/2013	Klein	03BL	Blog, Integrated into Site	$300.00	1	$300.00
3 /12/2013	Klein	06HR	Hourly Rate for Modificatior	$80.00	3	$240.00

Sum $2,740.00

The Group Footers show totals for Invoice Numbers 29 and 30.

InvNum 30

Invoice Date	Last Name	ProdID	Description	Price	Qty	LineTotal
3 /21/2013	Klein	06HR	Hourly Rate for Modificatior	$80.00	3	$240.00
3 /21/2013	Klein	02SP	Secondary Page	$200.00	1	$200.00
3 /21/2013	Klein	05IM	Image, Custom Designed	$40.00	2	$80.00

Sum $520.00

The Group Footer for Employee ID MJW adds the group totals for invoices 29 and 30.

Sum $3,260.00

Grand Total $19,920.00

Friday, February 12, 2016 Page 1 of 1

The Page Footer is often used for page numbers and dates.

The Grand Total appears in the Report Footer and adds all group totals (some not shown here).

Grouping and Sorting

A group is a collection of records that has at least one data element or key field in common. In the preceding example, records are grouped first by Employee ID MJW then by Invoice Numbers 29 and 30. A group consists of a header, records, and a footer. Grouping helps organize the information in meaningful ways.

It is important that records first be sorted using the same field that is used for grouping. Otherwise, a new group might be created each time the data in the group changes. Sorting can be added in the report; however, it's best to make the sorting occur in the underlying tables or queries.

The Report Wizard

The Report Wizard is a great way to get started with most reports. It lets you choose multiple tables or queries, group and sort data, perform calculations, and organize and present the information. The Wizard builds the report for you creating the necessary structure and organization.

Create→Reports→Report Wizard

DEVELOP YOUR SKILLS: A4-D2

In this exercise, you will create a detailed Invoice report using the Report Wizard.

1. Choose **Invoice Details Query Q1 2013** in the Navigation pane under the Queries heading.

2. Choose **Create→Reports→Report Wizard** .

   Invoice Details Query Q1 2013 is chosen in the Tables/Queries list because you chose it prior to starting the Report Wizard.

3. Double-click the **EmpID** field to add it to the **Selected Fields** list, or choose it and click the **Add** > button.

4. Add the **InvNum**, **InvDate**, **CustLastName**, **ProdID**, **Price**, **Qty**, and **LineTotal** fields to the **Selected Fields** list.

   Do not select CustFirstName and ProdDescription. If you add every field to the report, there won't be enough room to display all of the information. Be sure that EmpID is the first field on the list.

5. Click **Next**, and the Wizard will ask if you want grouping levels.

6. With **EmpID** selected, click the **Add** > button to set **EmpID** as the first grouping level.

   All invoices associated with a particular employee will be grouped together.

7. Now add the **InvNum** field to make it the second grouping level.

   The information will first be grouped by employee ID and then within each employee group by invoice number.

8. Click **Next**, and the sort order and summary information screen will appear.

   This is where you can add totals and other calculations and sort the results within groups. The underlying query sorts the invoices in ascending order so it isn't necessary to add sorting in this report.

9. Click the **Summary Options** button in the lower part of the dialog box.

   Price, Qty, and LineTotal are numeric fields, so they can be used to create totals as well as average, minimum, or maximum values.

10. Check the **Sum** box for the LineTotal field.

    This will sum up the invoices associated with each employee ID.

Field	Sum	Avg	Min	Max
Price	☐	☐	☐	☐
Qty	☐	☐	☐	☐
LineTotal	☑	☐	☐	☐

11. Leave the other settings as they are and click **OK**.

12. Click **Next** since sorting isn't needed.

13. Choose **Outline** as the Layout option and **Landscape** as the Orientation.

14. Leave the **Adjust the Field Width** box checked and click **Next**.

15. Name the report `Invoice Details Report Q1 2013` and click **Finish**.

16. Take a moment to review the report using the page controls at the bottom of the screen (there should be five pages).

    Your report displays in Print Preview, showing invoice totals and summary totals for each employee. The Report Wizard provides a great starting point; however, the report needs some formatting and layout work.

17. Click the **Close Print Preview** button on the right side of the Ribbon.

    The report will display in Design View.

Modifying Reports

Reports can be created from scratch using Design View but the Report Wizard is much easier to use and far more efficient. The Report Wizard provides a great starting point but it's often necessary to add, delete, move, or resize fields and to enhance a report in other ways such as adding titles and a company logo. These and other enhancements can be done using Layout View or Design View.

View the video "Modify Reports in Layout View."

View the video "Modify Reports in Design View."

Controls

Controls determine where field data, titles, headings, images, and other information are precisely positioned within report sections. There are three types of controls used in reports.

TYPES OF CONTROLS

Control Type	Description
Bound	Controls that display data from the table or query
Unbound	Objects that enhance the appearance of a report such as labels, titles, lines, and images
Calculated	Controls that display calculated fields from queries or that perform calculations within the report itself

The following controls are available on the Design tab of the Ribbon.

Available controls

Adding Fields to a Report

Sometimes fields need to be added to an existing report. The Existing Fields tool displays a list of tables and their fields. Fields are added to the report in Design View by dragging them from the Field List pane into report sections. Adding a field creates a text box control where the field data is displayed and a label control that contains the field name. The label can be changed, allowing you to be creative with the field names displayed on the report.

Design→Tools→Add Existing Fields

DEVELOP YOUR SKILLS: A4-D3

In this exercise, you will delete unneeded controls, add controls, and rearrange and resize controls to produce a more attractive, well-balanced report.

1. If necessary, open **Invoice Details Report Q1 2013**.

Delete, Align, and Size Controls

2. Switch to **Layout View** .

   Layout View lets you easily move controls and adjust their sizes while seeing how the report will look when printed.

3. Close any boxes that may be open such as the Property Sheet or Field List pane.
4. Follow these steps to delete and rearrange the invoice number summary controls:

Invoice Details Report Q1 2013

EmpID JFW

InvNum 20

Invoice Date	Last Name	ProdID	Price	Qty	LineTotal
1/5/2013	Smith	05IM	$40.00	14	$560.00
1/5/2013	Smith	06HR	$80.00	5	$400.00
1/5/2013	Sm	04SC	$400.00	1	$400.00

Summary for 'InvNum' = 20 (3 detail records)

Sum 1360

A B C D

A Click the **Summary for 'InvNum'** control and tap Delete to remove it.

B Click the **Sum** label then tap or hold the right arrow → to move it across the report next to the LineTotal box.

C With the Sum label still selected, press the Ctrl key and click the **total** box. Both controls should be selected.

D Tap the **up arrow** ↑ three times to move the controls up.

This section of the report should now look like this.

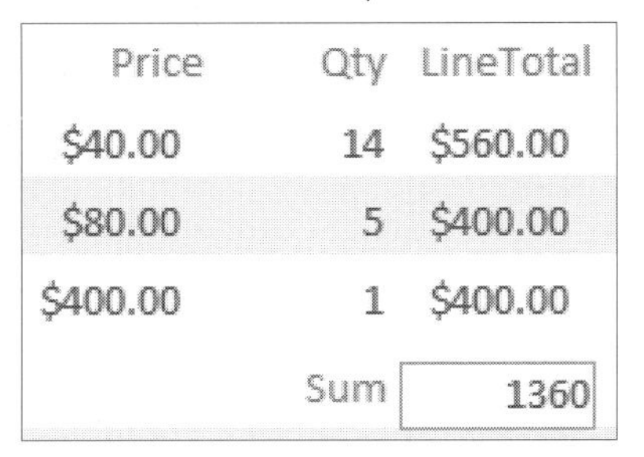

Price	Qty	LineTotal
$40.00	14	$560.00
$80.00	5	$400.00
$400.00	1	$400.00
	Sum	1360

ACCESS

5. Follow these steps to repeat the preceding procedure for the EmpID field controls:

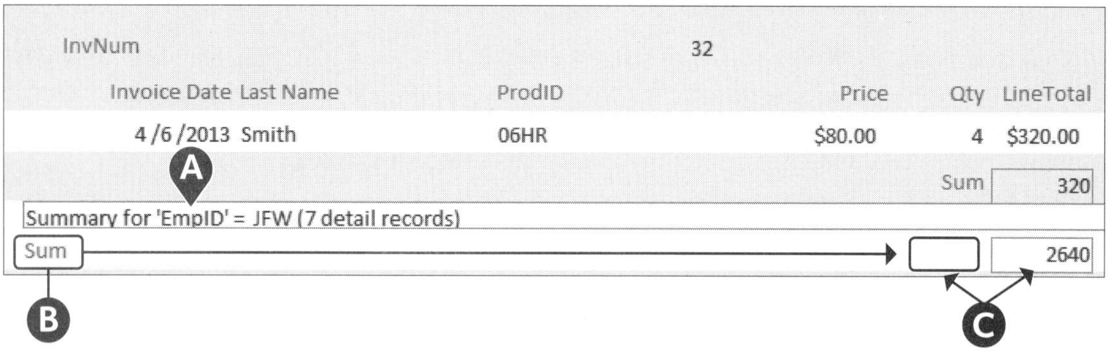

   A. Scroll down until *Summary for 'EmpID'* is visible, click to select it, and tap Delete to remove it.

   B. Scroll down, click the **Sum** label, and tap or hold the **right arrow** → until it is aligned with the Sum and Qty controls above it.

   C. With the Sum label selected, press the Ctrl key and click the **total** box, then tap the **up arrow** ↑ three times to move the controls up.

6. Follow these steps to change the width and alignment of the Price controls:

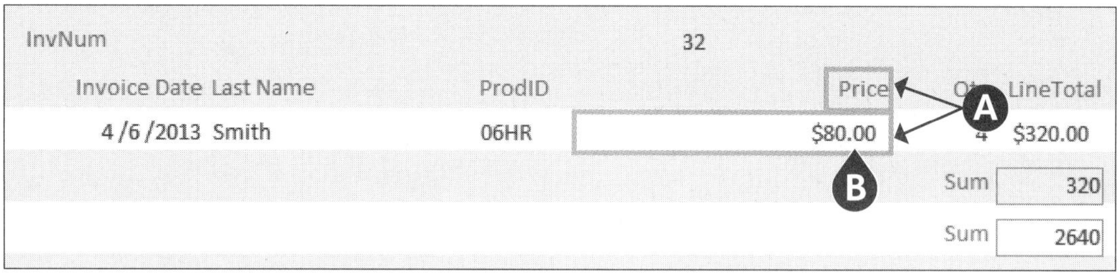

   A. Click any **Price** label and then tap the Ctrl key and click any **price** box to select all price labels and boxes.

   B. If the Property Sheet is not visible, right-click the selected controls and choose **Properties**.

7. Set the Width property to `0.8`.

   The setting won't take effect until you tap Enter or click in another box.

8. Set the Left property to `6.625` and tap Enter so you can see the change take effect.

   The Left property determines the position from the left side of the page. Now you will make changes in Design View.

Change the Width of a Control and the Overall Report

Now you will adjust the width of the page numbering control located in the Page Footer section.

9. Switch to **Design View**.

10. Click the **="Page"** numbering control located in the Page Footer section.

    You may need to move the Property Sheet box to be able to see the control. This control determines how page numbers appear in the report, including their position within the Page Footer.

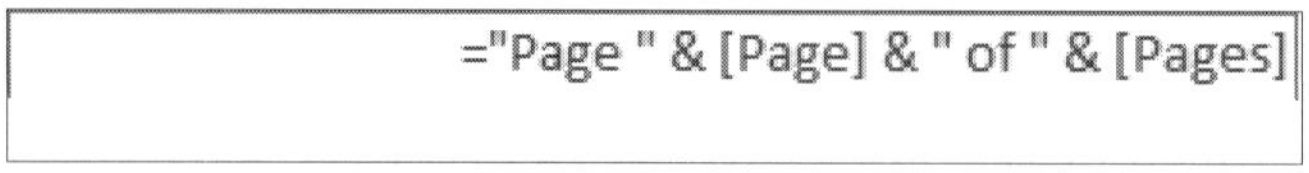

```
="Page " & [Page] & " of " & [Pages]
```

11. Make sure the Property Sheet box is visible, set the Width to **2**, and tap [Enter] to see the change.

Now you will change a width setting for the entire report.

12. Follow these steps to change the report width:

Property Sheet

Selection type: Report

Report (A)

Format | Data | Event | Other | All

Caption	Invoice Details Report Q1
Default View	Report View
Allow Report View	Yes
Allow Layout View	Yes
Picture Type	Embedded
Picture	(none)
Picture Tiling	No
Picture Alignment	Center
Picture Size Mode	Clip
Width	9" (B)
Auto Center	No
Auto Resize	Yes

(A) Click the **Selection Type** button in the Property Sheet box and choose **Report**.

(B) Set the Width to **9**.

You are now viewing the properties for the report rather than for individual controls. The overall report width will now be 9", although this won't be readily visible in Design View.

Add a Control

Now you will add the Product Description control to the report and reposition it and its label.

13. Choose **Design→Tools→Add Existing Fields**.

This tool lets you add new fields to reports.

14. Follow these steps to add the **ProdDescription** field and to move its label:

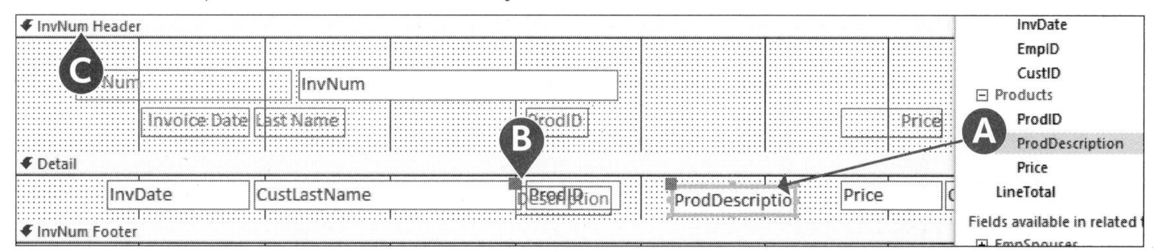

(A) Drag the **ProdDescription** field from the Field List pane and drop it between the ProdID and Price fields in the Detail section. It's important to place it in the Detail section.

(B) Right-click the new **ProdDescription** label (it will be hard to see) and choose **Cut** from the menu.

(C) Right-click the **InvNum** Header and choose **Paste**.

This will paste the field label in the header section. You will move it in the next step.

ACCESS

15. Follow these steps to reposition the fields:

Ⓐ Drag the **Description** label and drop it between the ProdID and Price labels in the InvNum Header.

Ⓑ Use the arrow keys to position the **Description** label and the **ProdDescription** field so they are left-aligned with one another and roughly centered between the ProdID and Price fields.

16. Close the Field List pane and switch to **Layout View**.

At this point, the top part of the report should closely match the following example. You will continue to enhance the appearance of this report.

Invoice Details Report Q1 2013

EmpID JFW

InvNum 20

Invoice Date	Last Name	ProdID	Description	Price	Qty	LineTotal
1/5/2013	Smith	05IM	Image, Custom	$40.00	14	$560.00
1/5/2013	Smith	06HR	Hourly Rate for	$80.00	5	$400.00
1/5/2013	Smith	04SC	Shopping Cart,	$400.00	1	$400.00

Sum 1360

Header and Footer Objects

The Header/Footer group on the design tab lets you easily add page numbers, titles, the date and time, and logos while working in Design View. Logos are especially useful as they can make reports look more professional and visually appealing. The Report Wizard only creates one report title, so the Title tool is often used to add subtitles.

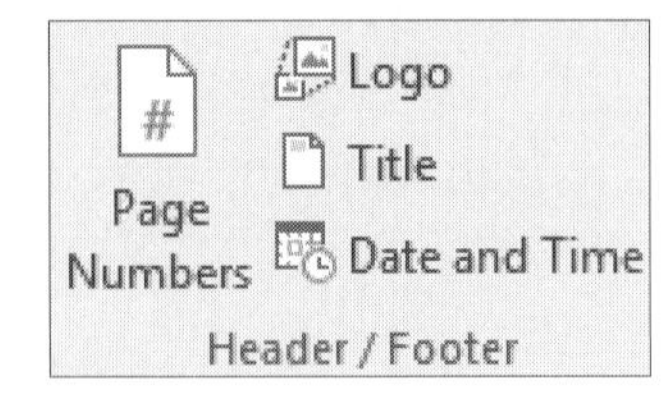

DEVELOP YOUR SKILLS: A4-D4

In this exercise, you will enhance the report header by adding a subtitle, logo, and the date and time, and you will format these controls.

1. Switch to **Design View**.

   The first thing you will do is increase the height of the header area to accommodate a logo and subtitle.

2. Right-click the **Report Header** section bar and choose **Properties**.

3. Set the Height property to **0.9**.

Modify and Format the Title

4. Click inside the current title box, **Invoice Details Report Q1 2013**, and replace the text with **Winchester Web Design**.

5. Set the properties for the title box as follows.

Property	Setting
Width	3.5
Font Size	22
Text Align	Center
Font Weight	Bold

Insert and Format a Subtitle

6. Choose **Design→Header/Footer→Title**.

   Notice the report name appears in the new title box, which is placed on top of the existing title.

7. Drag the new **subtitle** box so it is just below the *Winchester Web Design* title and aligned with it on the left side.

8. Replace the text in the new title box with **Invoices for Q1 2013**.

9. Set the properties for the new title as follows.

Property	Setting
Width	3.5
Height	0.35
Special Effect	Shadowed
Text Align	Center
Font Weight	Bold

Insert a Logo

10. Choose **Design→Header/Footer→Logo**, navigate to your **Access Chapter 4** folder, choose **WWD-Logo.bmp**, and click **OK**.

    Access places the logo in the upper-left corner of the Report Header section.

11. Set the Left property of the logo to **4**.

    The logo moves over to the 4" position.

12. Set both the Width and Height properties to **0.8**.

Add the Date and Time and Review the Report

13. Choose **Design→Header/Footer→Date and Time** .
14. Choose the **mm/dd/yyyy** date format (the third format).
15. Uncheck the **Include Time** checkbox and click **OK**.

    The date is inserted at the right edge of the header.

16. Switch to **Report View** and review your Report Header.

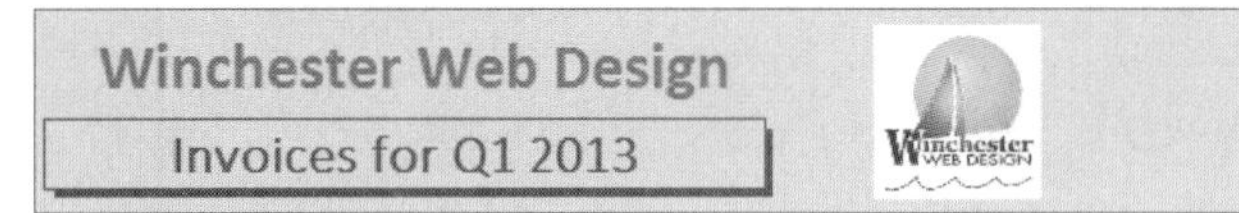

Formatting Controls

It is important to ensure that the data values are fully displayed in a report, while at the same time taking care not to leave unsightly and unnecessary blank space between columns. To accomplish this, you must resize, reposition, and align controls. It is best to adjust controls in Layout View because you can see the actual field values while making the adjustments. Multiple controls can be formatted together by first selecting them while using the Ctrl key.

DEVELOP YOUR SKILLS: A4-D5

In this exercise, you will use both Design View and Layout View to resize, reposition, and align report controls.

1. Switch to **Design View** in the **Invoice Details Report Q1 2013** report.
2. Click the **vertical ruler** to the left of the InvNum label and text box in the InvNum Header as shown here to select both of them.

    You can also click one field and hold down the Ctrl key while clicking the other.

3. Tap the **up arrow** ↑ five times to nudge the controls up closer to the InvNum Header.
4. Select the remaining controls in the InvNum Header section as shown here and tap the **up arrow** ↑ five times to nudge them up.

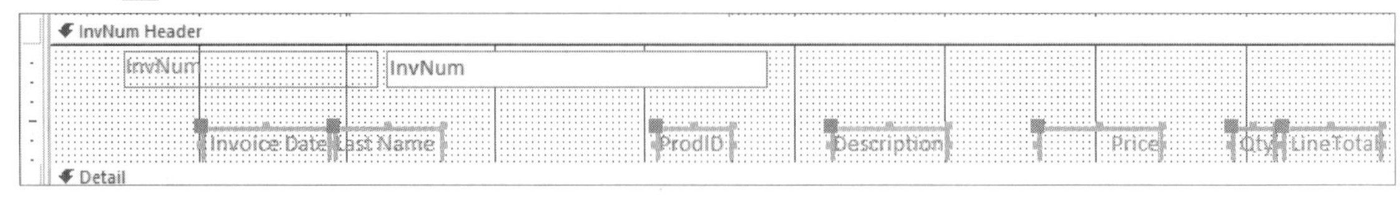

5. Position the mouse pointer on the top edge of the **Detail** section bar as shown here and drag it up until it is just below the controls you just moved.

6. If necessary, choose **Design→Tools→Property Sheet** to display the Property Sheet.
7. Select both of the **EmpID** controls in the EmpID Header section as shown here.

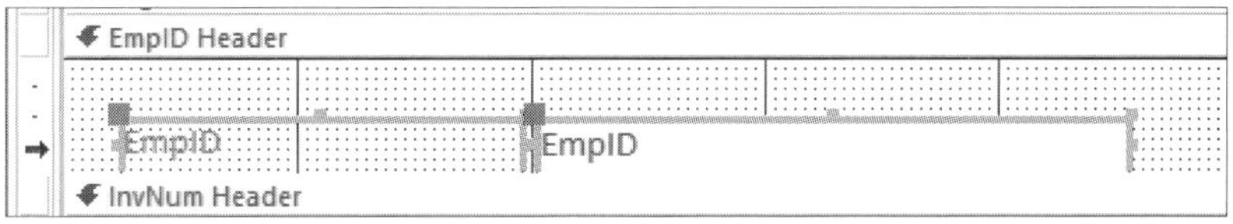

EmpID Header
EmpID EmpID
InvNum Header

8. Set the Top property for these controls to **0**.

   This will move them up so they are just below the EmpID Header. You can move controls by setting properties, using the arrow keys, or dragging. Setting properties is a way to position them with precision.

9. Click the **EmpID** Header and it will turn black, indicating it is selected as shown here.

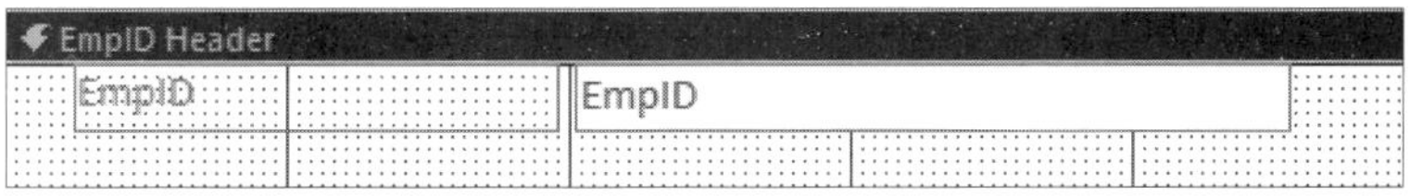

EmpID Header
EmpID EmpID

10. Set the Height property to **0.33**.

    Access sometimes changes a precise property value that you type, so don't worry if your Height property differs slightly from 0.33.

11. Switch to **Layout View**.
12. Click one of the **boxes** in the Description column to select all of the fields and then drag left to widen the column almost to the ProdID column.

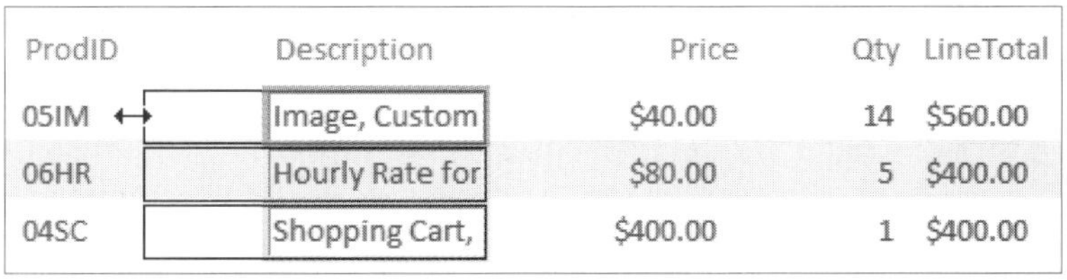

ProdID	Description	Price	Qty	LineTotal
05IM	Image, Custom	$40.00	14	$560.00
06HR	Hourly Rate for	$80.00	5	$400.00
04SC	Shopping Cart,	$400.00	1	$400.00

13. Select the **Last Name** boxes and drag left to shorten the boxes as shown here.

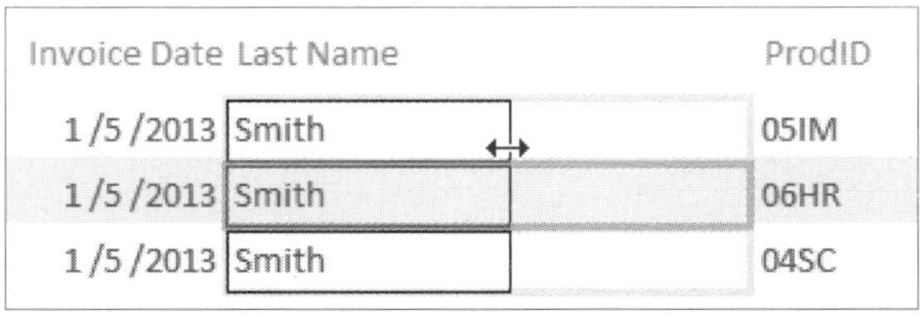

Invoice Date	Last Name	ProdID
1/5/2013	Smith	05IM
1/5/2013	Smith	06HR
1/5/2013	Smith	04SC

14. Press Ctrl and click the **Last Name** label to select the label and all the name boxes as shown here.

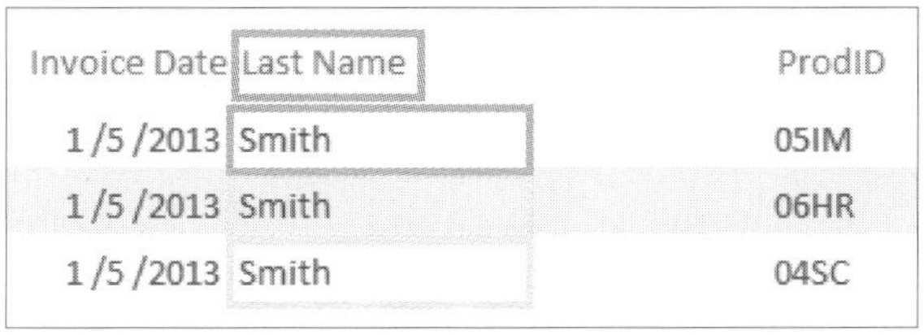

Invoice Date	Last Name	ProdID
1/5/2013	Smith	05IM
1/5/2013	Smith	06HR
1/5/2013	Smith	04SC

    In the next step, you will nudge the boxes to the right. Sometimes while moving a group of controls in Layout View, the screen scrolls down to the end. If this occurs, just keep nudging until you are finished and then scroll back up to the top of the report.

15. Tap the **right arrow** → eight times to nudge the boxes to the right.

16. Select the **ProdID** label and one of the boxes below it and then nudge the entire selection to the left six times.

17. Scroll to the top of the report and click the **InvNum** box with *20* in it then drag the left border to the right to shorten the box as shown here.

InvNum 20
Invoice Date Last Name ProdID

18. Tab the **left arrow** [←] enough times to position the box closer to the InvNum label as shown here.

InvNum 20
Invoice Date Last Name ProdID
1/5/2013 Smith 05IM

19. Scroll to the bottom of the report until the Sum controls are visible.

20. Use the [Ctrl] key to select the three **Sum** boxes and the **Grand Total** box as shown here.

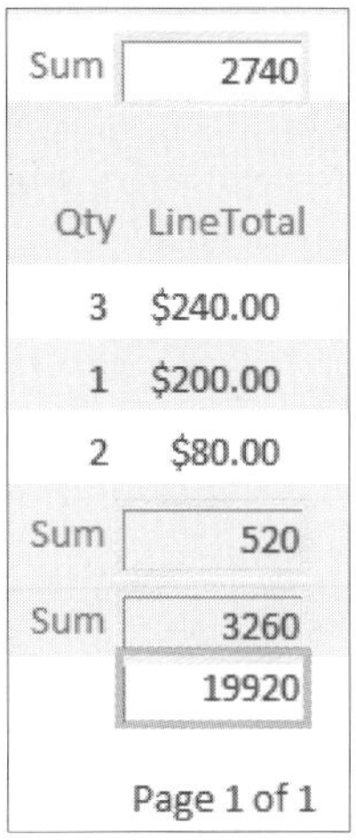

Sum 2740
Qty LineTotal
3 $240.00
1 $200.00
2 $80.00
Sum 520
Sum 3260
19920
Page 1 of 1

21. Set the Format property in the Property Sheet to **Currency**.

When you apply formatting, the fields may no longer fit in the text box. When a value is too large for the text box, it fills the box with the # symbol.

22. With the controls still selected, press [Ctrl] and click one of the currently unselected boxes in the column so that all line total boxes are selected as shown here.

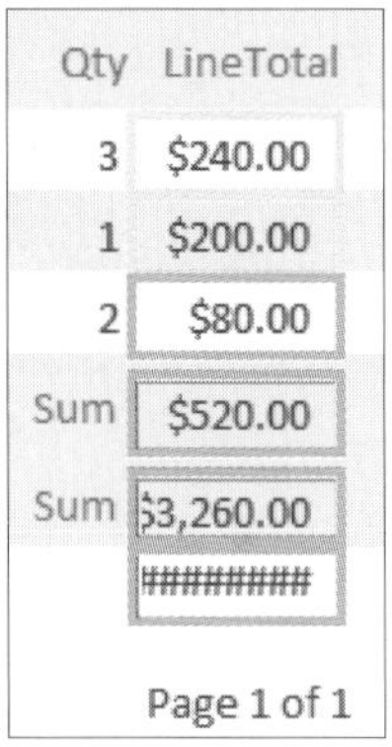

Qty LineTotal
3 $240.00
1 $200.00
2 $80.00
Sum $520.00
Sum $3,260.00
#########
Page 1 of 1

23. Now drag the right border of one of the controls to the right until the Grand Total is fully visible.

24. Switch to **Print Preview** view to see how your report will look when printed.
25. Close Print Preview and feel free to return to Design View or Layout View to make additional adjustments to the report.
26. Save the report.

Themes

Themes are prepackaged groups of design elements such as background colors, font families, font sizes, and other properties. When themes are applied they impact all objects in the database. The Themes group on the Ribbon lets you change the colors and fonts or the overall design.

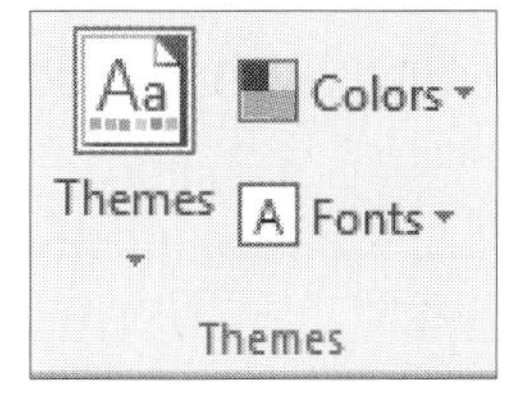

Design→Themes→Themes

DEVELOP YOUR SKILLS: A4-D6

In this exercise, you will apply a theme to your report.

1. Switch to **Design View** and choose **Design→Themes→Themes**.
2. Hover over each theme's thumbnail and notice how the report changes.

   Access themes are subtle, applying small incremental changes to the report.
3. Choose your favorite theme and then switch to **Print Preview** to see how your finished report will look with the new theme.
4. Choose **File→Close** to close the database, saving the changes to your report.

Self-Assessment

Check your knowledge of this chapter's key concepts and skills using the Self-Assessment in your ebook or eLab course.

Reinforce Your Skills

REINFORCE YOUR SKILLS: A4-R1

Create and Modify a Report

The president of Kids for Change wants a report that lists financial donations the organization has received since its inception, grouped by donor. He also wants to list the amount that K4C is depositing into its scholarship fund for local high school students. In this exercise, you will create a basic donations report and create a more customized report. Then, you will rearrange, resize, and format controls, and add a logo and title.

1. Start Access, open **A4-R1-K4C** from your **Access Chapter 4** folder, and save it as **`A4-R1-K4CRevised`**.

Create a Basic Report

2. If an Enable Content message appears, click it.

   Choose to enable the content if that message appears when opening any databases in this and other exercise projects.

3. Choose the **Donations** table in the Navigation pane.
4. Choose **Create→Reports→Report**.
5. Take a moment to review the report, save it as **`Quick Donations List`**, and then close it.

Create a Report Using the Report Wizard

Now you will create a donations report that is grouped by donor IDs and includes donation totals.

6. Choose **Donations Query** in the Navigation pane.
7. Choose **Create→Reports→Report Wizard**.
8. Add **DonorID**, **DonorLName**, **DonorFName**, **DonationDate**, and **Amount** to the selected fields list and click **Next**.

   The next Wizard screens asks how you want to view your data. This screen appears because the query uses two tables and the Wizard wants to know which table will be used for the first grouping level.

9. Choose **By Donations** and click **Next**.
10. Choose **DonorID** as the grouping field and add it to the grouping area.
11. Click **Next** then click the **Summary Options** button.
12. Check the **Sum** box for the Amount field and click **OK** to add a sum calculation for that field.
13. Click **Next** and the layout options screen will appear.
14. Choose **Block** for the layout and **Landscape** for the orientation.
15. Click **Next** to display the final Wizard screen.
16. Enter **`Donations Report 2013-2014`** as the title and click **Finish**.
17. Review both report pages and then close Print Preview.

    You will continue to use this report.

Add, Delete, and Edit Report Controls

18. In **Design View**, open the Property Sheet, if necessary.

In the next few steps you will select and format text boxes that display field data and the labels for those text boxes. The text boxes are located in the Detail section while their labels are located in the Page Header section.

Labels are in the Page Header section; text boxes are in the Detail section.

19. Click the **DonorID** text box in the Detail section and set the Width property to `0.5`.

20. Use the Ctrl key to select both the **DonorLName** and **DonorFName** text boxes in the Detail section and set the Width property to `1` to apply it to both controls.

21. Select the **Last Name** label in the Page Header section and the **DonorLName** text box in the Detail section and set their Left properties to `1.5`.

22. Select the **First Name** label in the Page Header section and the **DonorFName** text box in the Detail section and set their Left properties to `3`.

23. If necessary, scroll to the right of the report grid to see the other controls.

24. Choose the **Date** label in the Page Header section and set its Left property to `5`.

25. Choose the **DonationDate** text box in the Detail section and set its Left property to `4.5`.

26. Choose the **Amount** label in the Page Header and set its Left property to `6.2`.

27. Select the **Amount** text box in the Detail section and both **=Sum(Amount)** controls located in the DonorID Footer and in the Report Footer.

28. Set the Width property of the three controls to `1` and the Left property to `6`.

Add a New Field and Format It

29. Choose **Design→Tools→Add Existing Fields** to open the Field List pane.

30. Drag **ScholarFund** from the Field List pane and drop it to the right of the Amount text box in the Detail section.

The corresponding Scholar Fund label is partly on top of the Amount text box.

31. Click the **Scholar Fund** label and tap Delete to remove it.

Next you will use the Label control tool to insert a new label in the Page Header for the Scholar Fund.

32. Choose **Design→Controls→Label** Aa.

33. Drag the **Page Header** section above the ScholarFund text box to create a rectangular label box.

34. Type `Scholarship` into the new label, adjusting the size of the label box as necessary.

35. Close the Field List pane.

36. Scroll to the left in the design grid.

37. Click the long **Summary for " & "'DonorID'...** control in the DonorID Footer section.

38. Tap Delete to remove the control.
39. Click in the **Sum** label located in the DonorID Footer and replace the label text *Sum* with **Donor ID Total**.
40. Select the **title** in the Report Header section and replace it with **Kids for Change**.

Add a Logo and a New Title

41. Choose **Design→Header/Footer→Logo**, navigate to your **Access Chapter 4** folder, choose **K4C-Logo.bmp**, and click **OK**.
42. Set the Width and Height properties of the logo to **0.7**.
43. Drag the logo toward the right side of the header so it is positioned above the Amount fields.
44. Choose **Design→Header/Footer→Title**.
45. Drag the new title to the left and position it below the Kids for Change title.
46. Switch to **Report View** to see how your report looks.
47. If necessary, switch back to **Design View** and make adjustments to your report.
48. Close the database, saving the changes to your report.

REINFORCE YOUR SKILLS: A4-R2

Use Controls and Apply a Theme

In this exercise, you will size, align, and format report controls, apply a theme, and add the date to the Page Header.

1. Open **A4-R2-K4C** from your **Access Chapter 4** folder and save it as **A4-R2-K4CRevised**.

Size, Align, and Format Report Controls

2. Double-click the **Donations Report 2013-2014**.

   The report has some alignment problems, and the formatting of controls is inconsistent.

3. Switch to **Design View** and open the Property Sheet, if necessary.
4. Select the two titles in the Report Header section and set these property values as follows.

Property	Value
Width	4
Height	0.4
Left	2
Text Align	Center

5. Press Ctrl and click the *Donations Report 2013-2014* subtitle to deselect it.
6. Set the Font Size property of the *Kids for Change title* to **22**.
7. Set the Width and Height properties of the logo to **0.8**.
8. Set the logo's Top property to **0.05**.

   Be sure to type 0.05 *and not* 0.5.

9. Click the vertical ruler to the left of the controls in the Detail section to select all the controls in that section.

10. Choose **Arrange→Sizing & Ordering→Size/Space→Equal Horizontal** to evenly space all controls in the Detail section.
11. Click the **Last Name** label in the Page Header, press Ctrl, and click the **DonorLName** text box in the Detail section.
12. Choose **Arrange→Sizing & Ordering→Align→Left** to left-align the controls.
13. Follow the procedures in the previous two steps to left-align the First Name controls.
14. Click the **Date** label in the Page Header and drag it so it is centered above the DonationDate text box.
15. Select the **Donor ID Total** label (located in the DonorID Footer), the **Grand Total** label (located in the Report Footer), and the **DonationDate** text box (located in the Detail section).
16. Choose **Arrange→Sizing & Ordering→Align→Right** to right-align the controls.
17. Select the **Amount** text box located in the Detail section and the two **=Sum([Amount])** calculated controls located in the DonorID Footer and the Report Footer.
18. Choose **Arrange→Sizing & Ordering→Align→Right** to right-align the controls.

Add the Date to the Page Header

Now you will add a date control to the Page Header section so when viewing the report on a computer, readers don't have to scroll to the very end of the report to check the date.

19. Click **=Now( )** in the Page Footer section and tap Delete to remove it.
20. Choose **Design→Header/Footer→Date and Time**.
21. Choose the **mm/dd/yyyy** date format (the third format).
22. Uncheck the **Include Time** checkbox and click **OK**.

    The new date control is inserted on the right-hand side of the Report Header. You may need to move the Property Sheet to be able to see the new date box.

23. Click the **new date** control and set the following property values.

Property	Value
Width	1
Top	0.875
Left	3.5
Text Align	Center

24. Switch to **Print Preview** to review the completed report.
25. Feel free to return to **Design View** to make any adjustments you feel are necessary.
26. Close the report when you are finished, saving any changes.

Apply Themes to a Report

27. Display the **Quick Donations List** report in **Design View**.
28. Choose **Design→Themes→Themes** and apply the theme of your choice to the report.
29. Review the report in **Print Preview** and, if desired, switch back to **Design View** to choose another theme.
30. Save the report and close it when you're finished.

REINFORCE YOUR SKILLS: A4-R3

Create Reports and Modify Controls

Kids for Change (K4C) is rapidly expanding, adding new activities and staff members almost daily. To meet the organization's need to match staffers with the new activities, you will create two new reports for them.

1. Open **A4-R3-K4C** from your **Access Chapter 4** folder and save it as `A4-R3-K4CRevised`.

Create a Basic Report and Use Layout View

2. Choose the **Activities** table in the Navigation pane and then choose **Create→Reports→Report**.

   Access generates a report of K4C's activities in Layout View. Notice the vertical dotted line toward the right side of the report. This is a page break line indicating the report extends beyond a standard 8.5" x 11" printed page.

3. Click an **Activity** text box to select the entire Activity column of text boxes.
4. Hover the mouse pointer over the right border of one of the text boxes until it is a resize arrow.
5. Drag the **border** to the left to reduce the width of the text boxes to fit the widest entry in the column.
6. Resize the remaining columns to fit the widest entries in the columns.
7. Switch to **Design View** and display the Property Sheet.
8. Click the **="Page"** control located in the Page Footer.
9. Set the Width property to `1` and the Left property to `6`.
10. Choose **Report** from the Selection Type list at the top of the Property Sheet box and set the Width property to `7`.

    Access may change the property making it greater than 7 to account for any variations in your report. Setting this property to 7 adjusts the overall width of the report.

11. Select the **=Count(*)** control in the Report Footer and set the Height property to `0.175`.
12. Switch to **Print Preview**.

    The report should now fit nicely on one page.

13. Close Print Preview, save the report as `Activities Report`, and then close it.

Create a Report Using the Report Wizard

Now you will use the Report Wizard to create a staff availability report to match staffers with specific activities. The report will be grouped by activity.

14. Click the **Staff Schedule** query in the Navigation pane and then choose **Create→Reports→Report Wizard**.
15. Add the **Activity**, **Day**, **MeetTime**, **StaffLastName**, **StaffFirstName**, **StaffPhone**, and **Hours** fields to the Selected Fields list.
16. Click **Next** and add **Activity** as a group.

17. Click **Next** and then click **Next** again to skip the Sort Order and Summary screen.
18. Click **Next** again to accept Stepped as the layout.
19. Name the report **`Staff Availability Report`** and click **Finish**.

Size, Add, Delete, and Edit Report Controls

20. Close Print Preview and display the report in **Layout View**.
21. Open the Property Sheet, if necessary.
22. Select the **Activity** label and an **Activity** text box (Animal Shelter) and set the Width property to **`1.2`**.
23. Select the **Day** label and a **Day** text box.
24. Set the Width property to **`0.9`** and the Left property to **`1.5`**.
25. Set the Width property of the **Meet Time** label and boxes to **`0.75`** and the Left property to **`2.5`**.
26. Set the Width property of the **Last Name** label and boxes to **`0.8`** and the Left property to **`3.3`**.
27. Set the Width property of the **First Name** label and boxes to **`0.8`** and the Left property to **`4.2`**.
28. Set the Width property of the **Telephone** label and boxes to **`1.1`** and the Left property to **`5.1`**.
29. Set the Width property of the **Hours** label and boxes to **`0.4`** and the Left property to **`7`**.
30. Switch to **Design View**.
31. Choose **Design→Tools→Add Existing Fields** to display the Field List pane.
32. Drag the **HrlySal** field to the right of the **StaffPhone** text box in the Detail section.

    A label control is included with the text box. You will delete the label then add a new label in the Page Header section.
33. Click the **HrlySal** label control, which will be on top of the StaffPhone box, and delete it.
34. Close the Field List pane and open the Property Sheet.
35. Select the **HrlySal** text box and set the Width property to **`0.55`** and the Left property to **`6.3`**.
36. If necessary, use the arrow keys to nudge the control up or down to align it with the other controls in the Detail section.
37. Choose **Design→Controls→Label** *Aa* and drag a new label between the Telephone and Hrs labels in the Page Header section.
38. Type **`Hrly Sal`** in the new label and tap Enter.
39. Set the Width property of the new label to **`0.55`** and the Left property to **`6.3`**.
40. If necessary, use the arrow keys to nudge the control up or down to align it with the other controls in the Page Header section.
41. Switch to **Print Preview** to review your report.

Add a Subtitle and a Logo

42. Close Print Preview and switch to **Design View**.
43. Select the **title** in the Report Header and replace the text with **`Kids for Change`**.

44. Set the following property values for the Kids for Change title.

Property	Value
Width	4
Left	2
Font Size	22
Text Align	Center

45. Choose **Design→Header/Footer→Title** to insert a new title.
46. Enter the following property values for the new title.

Property	Value
Top	0.46
Width	4
Left	2
Font Size	20
Text Align	Center

47. Choose **Design→Header/Footer→Logo** and navigate to your **Access Chapter 4** folder.
48. Choose the **K4C-Logo.bmp** and click **OK** to insert it.
49. Set the Width and Height properties of the logo to **0.8**.

Add the Date to the Page Header Section

50. Choose **=Now()** in the Page Footer and delete it.
51. Choose **Design→Header/Footer→Date and Time**.
52. Choose the **mm/dd/yyyy** date format (the third format).
53. Uncheck the **Include Time** checkbox and click **OK**.

    The new date control is inserted on the right-hand side of the Page Header.
54. Click the **new date** control and tap the up arrow [↑] repeatedly to move it to the top of the Page Header section.
55. Drag the **left** border of the date box to the right to the 6.5" mark on the horizontal ruler.
56. Review your report using **Print Preview** and return to **Design View** to make any adjustments you feel are necessary.
57. Save the changes to your report and then close it.

Apply a Theme

58. Display **Activities Report** and take a moment to review it.
59. Switch to **Design View** and choose **Design→Themes→Themes**.
60. Choose a **theme** and switch to **Print Preview** to review the report with the new theme.
61. Switch back to **Design View** if you want to choose a different theme.
62. Close the database, saving the changes to your report.

Apply Your Skills

APPLY YOUR SKILLS: A4-A1

Create and Modify Reports

Universal Corporate Events, Ltd., is ready to add several reports to its database. In this exercise, you will create two reports: The first is a basic report that lists contacts' telephone numbers; the second lists the event venues and their contact information (address, telephone number, and website), grouped by the contact person. Then you will add, delete, and edit the venue report controls and also add a logo and title.

1. Open the **A4-A1-UCE** database from your **Access Chapter 4** folder and save it as **`A4-A1-UCERevised`**.

Create a Basic Report

2. Use the **Report** tool to create a report based on the **Contacts** table.
3. Save the report as **`Contacts List`** and then close it.

Use the Report Wizard and Delete and Edit Report Controls

Now you will use the Report Wizard to create a list of the event venues, including their address, phone number, and website, grouped by contact person.

4. Choose the **Venues** table and start the **Report Wizard**.
5. Choose all the fields *except* VenueID.
6. Leave VenueContact as the only grouping level.
7. Do not add a sort or change any layout options.
8. Name the report **`Venues List`** and finish the report.
9. Switch to **Design View** and delete the **=Now()** control in the Page Footer.
10. Change the *VenueContact* label in the Page Header to **`Contact`**.
11. Change the *VenueName* label in the Page Header to **`Name of Venue`**.

Add a New Title and a Logo

12. Change the *Venue List* title in the Report Header to **`Universal Corporate Events, Ltd.`** and then set the following properties for it.

Property	Value
Width	4
Height	0.4
Left	2
Font Name	Arial Narrow
Font Size	22
Text Align	Center

13. Insert a new title and leave the name set as *Venue List*.
14. Set the following properties for the new title.

ACCESS

Property	Value
Width	4
Height	0.4
Top	0.45
Left	2
Font Name	Arial Narrow
Font Size	20
Text Align	Center

15. Insert the **UCE-Logo.bmp** from your **Access Chapter 4** folder into the Header.

    The logo should be positioned on the left side of the header.

16. Set the logo's Width and Height to `0.8`.
17. Review your report in **Layout View**.

    The report has layout problems that are addressed in the next exercise.

18. Save the report, close it, and close the database.

APPLY YOUR SKILLS: A4-A2

Fine-Tune Reports

The CEO of Universal Corporate Events, Ltd., has sent back the first draft of the Contacts List and Venues List with a list of modifications he would like you to make. In this exercise, you will resize, align, and format controls on the Venues List report and apply a Theme to the Contacts List report.

1. Open the **A4-A2-UCE** database from your **Access Chapter 4** folder and save it as **`A4-A2-UCERevised`**.

Align Controls and Insert a Date

2. Display the **Venue List** report in **Layout View**.
3. Modify the position and width of all columns as necessary so that all data is visible.
4. Insert a date in the Header using the **mm/dd/yyyy** format and do not include the time.
5. Save the report and then close it.

Apply a Theme

6. Display the **Contacts List** report in **Design View**.
7. Apply a theme of your choice to the report.
8. View the report in **Report View** and make any adjustments you feel are necessary.
9. Save the report, close it, and close the database.

APPLY YOUR SKILLS: A4-A3

Create and Modify Reports

Universal Corporate Events, Ltd., is ready to add more reports to its database. In this exercise, you will create two reports: a basic report using the Menus table as the record source and a report that lists Personnel contact information grouped by last name. Then, you will add, delete, and edit report controls, modify the captions of several labels to make them more readable, and add a logo, title, and subtitle to the venue report.

1. Open the **A4-A3-UCE** database from your **Access Chapter 4** folder and save it as **`A4-A3-UCERevised`**.

Create Reports

2. Use the **Report** tool to create a report based on the **Menus** table.
3. Save the report as **`Menus List`** and close it.

   Now you will use the Report Wizard to create a list of the company personnel, their addresses, phone numbers, and email addresses. The report will be grouped by last name.

4. Choose the **Personnel** table and start the **Report Wizard**.
5. Add **PerLastName**, **PerFirstName**, **PerAddress**, **PerCity**, **ST**, **PerZIP**, **PerPhone**, and **PerEmail** to the **Selected Fields** list.
6. Use **PerLastName** as the only grouping level.
7. Do not add a sort, leave the layout default values, name the report **`Personnel List`**, and finish the report.

Modify Controls and Add a New Title, Logo, and Date

8. Switch to **Design View** and delete the **=Now()** and **="Page"** controls in the Page Footer.
9. Change the *PerLastName* label in the Page Header to **`Last Name`**.
10. Change the *Personnel List* title in the Report Header to **`Universal Corporate Events, Ltd.`**, and then set the following properties for it.

Property	Value
Width	4
Height	0.4
Left	2
Font Name	Arial Narrow
Font Size	22
Text Align	Center

11. Insert a new title and leave the name set as *Personnel List*.

ACCESS

12. Set the following properties for the new title.

Property	Value
Width	4
Height	0.4
Top	0.5
Left	2
Font Name	Arial Narrow
Font Size	22
Text Align	Center

13. Insert the **UCE-Logo.bmp** from your **Access Chapter 4** folder into the Header.

    The logo should be positioned on the left side of the header.

14. Set the logo's Width and Height to **0.8**.
15. Insert a date in the Header using the **mm/dd/yyyy** format and do not include the time.
16. Move the new **Date** control to the top right corner of the Report Header and shorten its width so it doesn't overlay the title.

Review the Report and Apply a Theme

17. Review your report in **Layout View**.

    Some controls such as Telephone and Email Address may not be wide enough to display all data. You will need to move some columns to the left to create space to allow for the expansion of the Telephone and Email Address columns. Remember that an entire column can be selected by clicking the column heading then using the Ctrl *key to select any box in the column.*

18. Move columns and widen columns as necessary so that all data is visible, but make sure that the Email Address field does not go past the vertical dotted page break line.
19. Save the report and close it.
20. Display the **Menus List** report in **Design View**.
21. Apply a theme of your choice to the report.
22. Review your report in **Report View** and change the theme if desired.
23. Save the report and then close it.

Extend Your Skills

These exercises challenge you to think critically and apply your new skills. You will be evaluated on your ability to follow directions, completeness, creativity, and the use of proper grammar and mechanics. Save files to your chapter folder. Submit assignments as directed.

A4-E1 That's the Way I See It

You've been asked to create a sales report for Blue Jean Landscaping that shows the total amount of sales by equipment type, drawing the information from sales invoices. Open **A4-E1-BJL** and save it as **A4-E1-BJLRevised**. Create a well-designed report header with a title and logo (use **BJL-Logo.bmp**). Make sure all information is visible and the report is easy to read and understand. The date and page numbering should appear at either the top or bottom of the report. Save your report as **Equipment Sales**.

A4-E2 Be Your Own Boss

Blue Jean Landscaping wants to add several reports to the company database that will provide listings of its equipment, services, and customers in an attractive and useful manner. Open **A4-E2-BJL** and save it as **A4-E2-BJLRevised**. Use the Store Inventory query as a record source to create a report that is grouped by manufacturer and includes item name, price, quantity in stock, inventory amount, and a sum of the InvTot field. Use the default layout settings. Use the skills you learned in this chapter to size, rearrange, and format the report controls. Create a well-designed report header with a title and logo (use **BJL-Logo.bmp**). Name the report **Store Inventory Report**. Create another report using the Service Invoices Query that includes all the fields except InvNum. Group the results by InvDate, sum the LineTotal field, choose the Stepped and Landscape layout options, and name the report **Service Invoices Report**. Format the report controls and create the same consistent header with a logo, title, and subtitle as in the Store Inventory Report.

A4-E3 Demonstrate Proficiency

You've been asked by Stormy BBQ to prepare a Manufacturer Stock Level report that shows the total number of items in stock for each manufacturer. Open **A4-E3-StormyBBQ** and save it as **A4-E3-StormyBBQ-Revised**. Locate the table or query in the database that will provide the data you need and use all fields from the table or query. Organize the report so the total stock for each manufacturer is displayed. Create a well-designed report Header with a title and logo (use **SBQ-Logo.bmp**). Make sure all information is visible and the report is easy to read and understand. The date and page numbering should appear at either the top or bottom of the report. Save your report as **Manufacturer Stock Levels**.

ACCESS

Glossary

controls Objects that display data, text, checkboxes, lines, images, or buttons

data Information such as names, numbers, dates, descriptions, etc., organized for reference or analysis

database A collection of data related to a particular subject or purpose, organized by records and fields; for example, an employee database contains information for each employee, such as their name, employee ID, and contact information

Datasheet View Displays actual data values

description Optional field property that may be used in Design View to help identify special information about a field

Design View Where form, query, and report layout is defined; shows field names and labels, as well as other objects that can be displayed

detail section Main section of a form or report that contains the text boxes that display data from underlying database tables; detail content varies from record to record

field A group or category of specific information or data, such as last names or phone numbers; in an Access table, each field is displayed in a column

foreign (or secondary) key Field in a secondary table that links to the primary key field in the main table, which contains the detailed information for a particular item

form Database screen used to enter, edit, and view data for an individual record in a layout that is more convenient and attractive than a table datasheet layout

Form Footer Bottom section of a form that appears on the last page of a page form; seldom used

Form Header Top section of a form that contains constant information, such as a title, logo, decorative line, or color scheme

group Collection of controls or records that have at least one feature in common; quick forms tie all automatically inserted text boxes and corresponding labels into one group, allowing you to move the entire group but not the individual controls; or, if you want to display all vendors with offices in the same state, you could group on the State field

Group Footer Displays the summary for a grouped field, such as the total of each employee's sales, grouped by the EmpID

Group Header Identifies a field (such as EmpID) by which report data is grouped, so a summary (such as a total of each employee's sales) can be displayed for the grouped field

labels Part of a control that contains a caption identifying the data displayed in a text box or checkbox; e.g., the caption Last Name is a good label for the LastName field

Layout View Combines the editing ability of Design View with the layout look of Form/Report View so you can better visualize and modify the form's appearance; does not allow you to add, change, or delete records

Navigation pane Objects panel that lists existing database objects (specifically tables, queries, forms, and reports)

object A database structure used to store or reference data

primary key Unique ID that cannot be the same for any two records (e.g., a student ID)

property Field attributes that control features such as format, field size, font size, weight, and color; available properties depend on the data type

Property Sheet Panel on the right side of a design window used to set values for controls, such as font size, color, alignment, etc., depending on the type of control

query Object used to select, search, sort, and extract table data based on criteria and conditions; displays results in a row-and-column format

real-time data Data that is updated and shown at the speed at which a computer receives and processes information

record Collection of details (fields) about an individual person, place, or thing, such as an employee record or a product record

record source Field property that connects text boxes in a form, subform, or report to a field in an underlying table or query

referential integrity Relationship protocol that maintains the validity of related data; requires that the data types of related primary and foreign key fields are the same or compatible

report Database page that presents processed and summarized data from tables and queries as meaningful information in an easy-to-read format; designed to be printed

sections The major parts of the form, such as the Form Header, Form Footer, Detail, Page Header, and Page Footer, that are separated by section bars

sort Process used to arrange data in a specific order, such as alphabetic, numeric, by date, or in ascending or descending order

split form Two synchronized views of a table data in Layout/Form View and Datasheet View, shown simultaneously

tab order Order in which Access moves among form fields when you press Tab or Enter

table A file or collection of related records; contain the data used in all other database objects

text boxes Controls that display the actual data stored in a field (e.g., Smith might be the data displayed in a LastName text box linked to the LastName field in an Employees table)

wildcards Special characters, such as an asterisk (*) used to represent multiple characters or a question mark (?) to represent any single character

Wizard Tool that walks you through the selection and ordering of specific fields from the tables or queries that contain the data you want to place onto a form, query, or report

work area Main part of the screen where you design tables, queries, forms, and reports; where you enter data into tables and forms

Index

Note: Index entries ending in "V" indicate that a term is discussed in the video referenced on that page.

SYMBOLS

* (asterisk) wildcard character, using, 46
[] (open/close brackets) wildcard characters, using, 46
? (question mark) wildcard character, using, 46

A

Access app. *See also* databases; relational databases
- AND/OR criteria, 46–47
- calculated fields, 50–52
- criteria in queries, 44–48
- date criteria, 47–48
- filtering table data, 11
- importing data sources, 12
- importing Excel worksheets, 16–17
- Layout View, 9
- limiting results returned, 49–50, 55
- modifying reports, 68–77
- report organization and structure, 65–67
- reports, 64–65
- Return feature, 49
- select queries, 40–44
- showing results, 49–50
- sorting results, 49–50
- sorting table data, 11
- tables, 6–10

Access databases. *See* databases
Access forms. *See* forms
Access window, contents, 3–6
AND/OR criteria, using, 46–47, 54, 58
asterisk (*) wildcard character, using, 46

C

calculated fields. *See also* fields
- adding and formatting, 59–61
- using, 50–52, 55–57, 59

control properties, setting, 27
controls
- formatting, 36–37
- reorganizing in Layout View, 24V

criteria in queries, using, 56–58

D

data files, 2
data normalization, 13–14
data sources, importing, 12
database objects, 3, 4V, 5–6
database work area, 4V
databases. *See also* Access app; relational databases
- creating tables in, 7–8
- creating, 18
- features, 2
- opening and saving, 3
- real-time data, 2–3
- types, 2–6

Datasheet View, 4, 15
date criteria, using, 47–48, 54–55, 57, 59
date field, 45
Design View, 15–16
- adding tables in, 17
- changing forms, 26–30
- creating queries in, 53, 56
- creating tables, 9–10
- features, 5
- modifying reports, 65, 67–72
- multi-table queries, 58

detail section
- modifying in forms, 35
- setting control properties, 27

E

editing, labels, 36

F

field data types, 7
field properties, 9–10
fields. *See also* calculated fields
- in Access tables, 6–7
- including in queries, 43
- for query criteria, 45
- selecting in Access tables, 43

filtering data in Access tables, 11
footers. *See* headers and footers
Form Footers, 26
Form Headers, 26, 37
form titles
- adding, 33
- setting properties, 27

Form Wizard, 23–24, 32
formatting
- calculated fields, 59–61
- controls, 36–37
- labels, 36

forms, 3–5
- adding titles and images, 33
- changing in Design View, 26–30
- changing in Layout View, 24–26
- controls, 23
- creating, 22–24, 37
- creating and arranging controls, 34
- creating and modifying, 35
- detail section, 24
- editing and formatting titles, 32
- labels, 24
- modifying header section, 35
- multiple-item type, 30–31
- sections, 24
- split type, 31
- tab order, 28
- text boxes, 24

H

header section, modifying in forms, 35
headers and footers, in reports, 65, 72–73

I

images, adding to forms, 33
importing
- data sources, 12
- tables, 18–19
- worksheets, 16–17, 19

L

labels
- in Access forms, 32–33
- editing and formatting, 36
- editing in forms, 24
- repositioning in forms, 25–26

Layout View, 9
- Access reports, 82
- changing Access forms, 24–26
- reorganizing controls in, 24V

logos, inserting in forms, 27–28, 32, 37

M

multiple item forms, creating, 30–31, 33
multi-table queries, creating, 53–54, 56, 58

N

Navigation pane in Access window, 3
Numeric & Currency field, 45

O
objects, 3–4
open/close brackets ([]) wildcard
characters, 46
OR criteria. *See* AND/OR criteria

P
primary key fields, 7
Property Sheets, using, 26, 27, 28

Q
queries, 3–5. *See also* select queries
creating, 53, 58
designing using tables, 43
features, 40–41
field types, 45
including fields in, 43
using criteria in, 44–48
query criteria, searching, 45
Query Design View, using, 42V, 43
query fields, rearranging, 43
query results, limiting and sorting, 49, 55, 57, 59
Query Wizard, using, 53, 56, 58
question mark (?) wildcard character, using, 46

R
record sources, 22
records in Access tables, 6
limiting and sorting, 60
limiting number displayed, 49–50, 59
referential integrity, 13
relational databases, 13–14, 17–19. *See also* Access app; databases
Report button, using, 64
report objects, 3–4
Report Wizard, using, 66–67, 78, 82–83, 85
reports, 5–6
adding controls, 71–72
adding date and time, 74
adding date to page header, 81
adding fields, 68–69
adding logos and titles, 73, 80
adding themes, 81
aligning controls, 69–70, 86
applying themes, 88
bound controls, 68
calculated controls, 68
changing width of controls, 70–71
controls and themes, 80–81
controls, 68, 83
creating and modifying controls, 82–84
creating and modifying, 78, 85, 87
date on page header, 84
deleting and editing controls, 85
deleting controls, 69–70
formatting controls, 74–77
grouping and sorting, 66
header and footer objects, 72–73
headers and footers, 65
inserting dates, 86
Layout View, 82
modifying, 68V
modifying controls, 79–80
reviewing, 74, 88
sections, 65–66
sizing controls, 69–70
subtitles and logos, 83–84
themes, 77, 84, 86
titles, logos, and dates, 87–88
titles and logos, 85–86
unbound controls, 68

S
saving, databases, 3
select queries, 40–44, 56, 59. *See also* queries
sizing, text boxes in forms, 24–25
sorting
query results, 49, 55, 57, 59
reports, 66
table data, 11
split forms, creating, 31

T
tab order in forms, 28
tables, 3–8, 15, 18–19
and queries, 43
in Design View, 9, 17
text boxes
in forms, 24–25, 32–33
repositioning in forms, 25–26
Text field criteria, 45
themes, 77
in forms, 29–30

W
wildcard characters, using, 46, 53–54, 57–60
work area, 3–4
worksheets, importing, 16–19

NOTES

NOTES

NOTES

NOTES

NOTES

NOTES

NOTES

NOTES

NOTES

NOTES

NOTES

NOTES